PENGUIN BOOKS

TALES OUT OF SCHOOL

Patrick Welsh was born in Batavia, New York, in 1941. He received his A.B. from Canisius College and his J.D. from George Washington University. He has been an English teacher for fifteen years, and lives in Alexandria, Virginia, with his wife and three children.

Dan Morgan has covered the national education story for *The Washington Post*. His last book was *Merchants of Grain*.

TALES
OUT OF SCHOOL

A Teacher's Candid Account from the Front Lines of the American High School Today

PATRICK WELSH

With an Introduction by Dan Morgan

ELISABETH SIFTON BOOKS
PENGUIN BOOKS

ELISABETH SIFTON BOOKS • PENGUIN BOOKS
Viking Penguin Inc., 40 West 23rd Street,
New York, New York 10010, U.S.A.
Penguin Books Ltd, 27 Wrights Lane, London W8 5TZ
(Publishing & Editorial) and Harmondsworth,
Middlesex, England (Distribution & Warehouse)
Penguin Books Australia Ltd, Ringwood, Victoria, Australia
Penguin Books Canada Limited, 2801 John Street,
Markham, Ontario, Canada L3R 1B4
Penguin Books (N.Z.) Ltd, 182–190 Wairau Road,
Auckland 10, New Zealand

First published in the United States of America by
Viking Penguin Inc. 1986
Published in Penguin Books 1987

Portions of this book first appeared in *The Washington
Post* in a slightly different form.

Grateful acknowledgment is made for permission to reprint
the following copyrighted material:
Excerpt from "The Writer" by Richard Wilbur.
Copyright © 1972 by Richard Wilbur. Reprinted from
his volume *The Mind Reader* by permission of
Harcourt Brace Jovanovich, Inc.
Excerpt from "Cherry Log Road" by James Dickey.
Copyright © 1963 by James Dickey. Reprinted from
Helmets by permission of Wesleyan University Press.

Excerpt from "Born Yesterday" from *The Less Deceived* by
Philip Larkin. By permission of The Marvell Press, London.

LIBRARY OF CONGRESS CATALOGING IN PUBLICATION DATA
Welsh, Patrick.
Tales out of school.
"Elisabeth Sifton books."
1. T. C. Williams High School (Alexandria, Va.)
2. Welsh, Patrick. 3. Education, Urban—Virginia—
Alexandria. I. Morgan, Dan. II. Title.
[LD7501.A4498.W45 1987]   373.755'296   86-21258
ISBN 0 14 00.9442 3

Printed in the United States of America by
R. R. Donnelley & Sons Company, Harrisonburg, Virginia
Set in Trump Mediaeval

To all my students
and my best teachers:

Angela
Neil
Claire
Magin

Introduction

This is a book that went in search of an author and found one.

In the fall of 1983, while working as an editor of the Sunday "Outlook" section of *The Washington Post*, I began looking for a teacher to write about life inside a large metropolitan high school. Interest in education was increasing; blue-ribbon panels were issuing all kinds of proposals for improving the nation's public schools, and state legislatures were passing many new laws to "reform" education. But all too predictably, it seemed to me, the discussion was being monopolized by "the experts"—people with advanced degrees and exalted titles sitting in the nation's universities, state departments of education, and think tanks. There seemed to be little or no place in the debate for ordinary, everyday parents, students, and, above all, teachers. I wanted to find somebody who could describe what is good and bad about schools from the perspective of the classroom, the cafeteria, and the PTA meeting. This book, which grew out of a series of nine articles that appeared in the *Post* in 1983–84, is the final result.

Before I met Pat Welsh, I was doubtful whether a teacher would take on the assignment I had in mind. Would he or she be willing to "tell tales out of school"? Would a teacher write candidly about other teachers, school administrators, parents, and students? And would such a teacher's bosses—his principal and superintendent—permit him or her to do so? Those questions were swirling around in my mind the day I drove out to meet Welsh, an English teacher I'd heard about from a friend. His school was T. C. Williams High, a sprawling, '60s-era brick-and-glass facility located at the edge of a busy suburban strip of low-rise office buildings and fast-food shops in Alexandria, Virginia.

Arriving in Welsh's classroom, I was greeted by a handsome but slightly rumpled man in his early forties. There was no chalk dust on his tweed jacket, but I noticed that his shirttail had come untucked in back. Books and papers were piled in a heap on his desk, and there were some papers on the floor. I came straight to the point. Would he be willing to explore the "anthropology" of his school? Could he give our readers an inside look at race relations, school politics, teachers' unions, and parents? I gave him some articles that the *Post* had published about a remote village in India. In order to describe the complicated politics and culture of the village, the British journalist Victor Zorza had cut his European ties and taken up a simple life there. His dispatches were filled with wonderfully detailed portraits of village headmen and revealing descriptions of the Indian caste system. These articles, I suggested to the astonished Welsh, might serve as a useful model for an insider's report on an American public high school.

Bewildered as he must have been by this, Welsh gamely agreed to take on the assignment, and he promised to complete the draft of his first article within several weeks. Then we walked back to meet the principal, Tony Hanley, an easygoing man with prematurely silver hair. Hanley was enthusiastic. His only request was to see drafts of what Welsh was writing—not to censor anything but to provide insights on aspects of school life with which Welsh, a classroom teacher, wouldn't ordinarily be familiar.

Pleased as I was to have found Pat, I was also excited about T. C. Williams High School. T.C., as everybody called it, served the community of Alexandria, Virginia, an old Southern town on the banks of the Potomac River that was only gradually being absorbed into the culture of metropolitan Washington. In many respects, it was a typical suburban institution. It was big: 2,400 students in grades ten through twelve, 170 teachers, hundreds of courses, dozens of extracurricular activities. Part of its clientele was from Washington's suburban elite: well-to-do middle-class families, many with two incomes from good government jobs, most with high ambitions for their children. They were part of America's "new middle class": the achievement-oriented, upwardly mobile families who want and expect the best of everything, from homes and vacations to education for their children. T.C.'s Class of '86 boasts 15 National Merit Scholarship Semi-Finalists, the second highest number of any school in the state.

Yet in other ways, T.C. was a typical *urban* school. More than half its students were black, culturally and economically disadvantaged or newly arrived immigrants. Alexandria had been in the thick of the desegregation battles of the previous three decades. Then it had become home for Asians and Latin Americans who came in the great wave of people taking advantage of relaxed American immigration laws in the '70s. T.C., whose corridors teemed with poor blacks, affluent whites, Afghans, and Salvadorans, provided a decisive test of America's vast social gamble on integration.

As I got to know Pat better, working with him first on the series and later on this book, I came to understand why he could write about this school in a way that no professional education expert or journalist ever could. Whatever faults he found with the school, teaching was more than a job to him. He had, I discovered, passed the Virginia Bar exam in the early '70s, but chose to continue teaching rather than take up a more lucrative career as a lawyer. Raised in a warm

Catholic family in upstate New York, Pat instinctively reached out to young people. He never told his students that he had spent three years in a Jesuit seminary. But it seemed to me that Pat came to the secular business of teaching as he might otherwise have come to the priesthood: as a way of having a "flock."

It wasn't long into our acquaintanceship before another aspect of Pat's character emerged. He was a storyteller, with an earthy vocabulary and a gift for the revealing anecdote. His descriptions of his teacher's milieu were often irreverent. He knew that teaching was the art of the possible, and that high school was a place where hormones were always more relevant than Homer. What set Welsh's writing apart from that of the education experts who were telling the world what was wrong with America's schools was his candor and utter honesty. He had the courage to acknowledge that some teachers do their best to avoid the "dumb" kids; that school administrators tolerate incompetent instructors rather than face a confrontation with the teachers' union; that many students are bored; and that parents seem to know almost nothing about their children's exploits with sex and drugs.

Pat could be cynical about the bureaucracy, the school administration, other teachers. But less often about the kids. For months I wondered why, exactly, parents so consistently described Pat as a good teacher. Was it his great intellect? His burning insights into literature? His exceptional skills as a motivator? Or was it perhaps his pride and sense of competition? Certainly his students did well on national tests. After watching Welsh at work in his classroom, I concluded that there is more to it than any of the above. I decided that Pat is good because he cares deeply about his students and it shows. That sounds almost trite. Yet I believe it is an uncommon quality that all too often is absent in big public schools. Welsh's students sense that they are being taught by an adult who does not consider them to be just moving parts in the great assembly line of education. It's that simple.

A teaching style, like a style of writing or painting, grows out of an individual's character and personality. I would describe Pat's as gentle and encouraging. (In fairness, I should mention an Irish temper that he claims to display from time to time, but which I never witnessed.) A Welsh class has an overall structure and direction, but leaves a lot of room for the students. Sitting in his classroom, I felt more conscious of the students than of Welsh, who would move around the room throwing out quick questions, then stand back to listen and watch intently. In the pauses, he would offer encouragement. "Good." And sometimes, "Dynamite!"

To teach in the kind of school T. C. Williams is requires a remarkable ability to change pace, to adjust to the drastically different abilities of students who come and go in fifty-minute sequences. In a first-period honors class attended mostly by white, middle-class kids, Welsh is a college instructor, reading fragments of students' writing, joking easily and apologizing for "playing English teacher" as he asks about the symbolism in *A Streetcar Named Desire*.

In a fourth-period class in which the students are as much as four years behind in their reading, Welsh is the traditional schoolmaster; he calls for quiet half a dozen times and warns one student to calm down or get out. All the students are black, except for one girl whose whiteness seems strikingly emphasized by the nurse's uniform she is wearing. One girl is very overweight. Another student turns his chair to face the rear of the classroom and keeps it like that for the duration. In the back row, a girl tweaks the chin of a guy in front of her. There are some tough kids in this class. Willy has been kicked out of several schools, the last time for smashing the teeth of a classmate with braces. As the hour progresses, Welsh deftly leads the group into a discussion of *Streetcar*, using scenes from the movie that he shows on a VCR. The kids have a good intuitive understanding of the issues involved in the complex, charged relationship between Stanley Kowalski and his sister-in-law, Blanche. While somebody in the honors course had commented that Stanley's behavior "couldn't happen nowadays," the fourth period students seem to have a better instinctive feel for Stanley's hostility toward Blanche. Willy advances his own theory: Stanley is "loved out"—street vernacular for having had too much "love boat," a mixture of marijuana and PCP. After a few minutes, the commotion has subsided and the students seem genuinely involved in the class.

Assistant Principal Bob Frear describes Welsh, the writer, as a "gentle muckraker." What he means is that Pat, in his quiet way, is in the tradition of reporters who look beneath the surface. And that is surely one thing that makes this book different from the volumes that have been published in recent months and years about schools.

By 1985, the idea of major educational reform was rolling ahead like a truck going downhill with no brakes. Forty-eight states were considering tougher high school graduation requirements and thirty-five had approved changes; twenty-one reported initiatives to improve textbooks; eight had approved longer school days; twenty-four were examining proposals to create "master teachers"; and thirteen were considering limiting extracurricular activities of students with academic problems.

The worthy goal of all these new requirements and regulations was to raise standards and improve academic achievement. But there was something troubling about the measures that were being so hastily adopted. In responding to the public concern about declining test scores and lax school discipline, state legislatures were coming forward with solutions that often seemed mechanistic and simplistic. These included such initiatives as mandating longer school days, reestablishing dress codes, and resurrecting that old standby, "more science and math."

As Welsh makes clear, such reforms cannot by themselves achieve the desired results. This is because the "crisis" is not just a school crisis, but a deeper one in American society. It relates to profound changes that have occurred in the lives and values of families; to a technological revolution that has totally altered the way that information and knowledge are transmitted and absorbed, especially by youth; and to upheavals caused by the remarkably rapid desegregation of our institutions in the '60s and '70s. Until the *whole* society acknowledges the depth and complexity of these changes, it is not likely that high schools appropriate to America's changed circumstances will emerge. As Prof. A. Harry Passow of Columbia Teachers College has written: "Reforming schools is very different from reforming society. Yet both must occur simultaneously if real reform of the education system is to take place."

Welsh's book tells the tale of how one American high school is trying, not always successfully, to cope with the immense forces that have changed America in the last two decades. It is, truly, a view from the front lines, and can help extend the debate about schools to those *in* the schools. In the last analysis, educational reform is too important to be left to the experts. It must have the serious, considered attention of parents, who need and expect very different things from high schools today than their parents did. And it requires the considered advice of those who are in the best position to know what does and does not work: gifted classroom teachers such as Pat Welsh. If this book does no more than begin opening up the discussion to those who have the most at stake in it, it will be a worthwhile contribution.

DAN MORGAN
Washington, D.C.

Contents

Tales Out of School

1

How Good Are We?

In January 1984, my high school was honored with a visit from the top education official in the land. Secretary of Education Terrel Bell drove across the Potomac River and presented T. C. Williams High School with one of the Reagan administration's first Excellence in Education awards. It was a major media event, and our school administrators made the most of it. On stage with Bell and Principal Robert A. Hanley in our small, ceremonial auditorium were the mayor, school superintendent and members of the city council and school board.

For the previous nine months, Bell had been proclaiming that America was a "nation at risk" because of its deteriorating high schools. But on this day, the Secretary was extolling T.C. as an example to the nation. He praised it as a school that was able to "meet the needs of all its students" in spite of the diversity of the student body. We were one of eighty-eight schools receiving an excellence award. Yet if the list had been cut to a mere ten, Bell assured us, "T. C. Williams would still be there."

Halfway through the speech I noticed that some of my fellow teachers had begun to chuckle quietly.

"Did you ever hear such bull in your life?" whispered a colleague.

"If we're in the top ten, can you imagine what some of the *rest* are like," said another.

"You gotta hand it to Hanley; he really snowed that government evaluation team," whispered somebody else.

1

When Bell referred to "my friend, Bob Hanley," there was a ripple of laughter. Everybody calls him Tony.

It wasn't that we were ungrateful for the recognition. Far from it. We wanted and needed it. A good image in the community was essential as we struggled to keep the support of Alexandria's middle-class families in the face of competition from private schools. None of us wanted T.C. to be just a place for the poor and disadvantaged. Each year we brandished our National Merit Scholarships, Ivy League acceptances, and science prizes to persuade anxious, middle-class parents that their children could get as good an education at the local public high school as at the expensive, mostly white private schools. The word in the community was that T.C. was an excellent place for the bright, motivated student. Private schools simply couldn't match our beautifully-equipped science laboratories, our array of college-level "advanced placement" courses, or our extensive sports and extra-curricular programs.

Yet those of us listening to Bell knew that, like most high schools, public and private, we took too much credit for the accomplishments of our many bright, motivated kids. As Bell went on with his speech, I wondered if he had any notion of the other side of the coin. His glorification of our school seemed as unrealistic as the condemnation that was constantly being heaped on the nation's public schools by committees of experts.

I doubted that Bell knew he had been invited to address only teachers and administrators after school, rather than the student body, because we always feared that large gatherings of our diverse pupils would get out of hand, causing an incident that might tarnish our image.

Did the Secretary know that the $5 million Career Wing in which the ceremony was being held had become a dumping ground for semiliterate black and foreign kids, some of whom were learning only such minimal skills as tire busting or stacking boxes?

Was he aware that many of the teachers in the audience were in despair about their failure to reach the half of the student body that reads below grade level, and that others simply refused to teach these substandard readers—and got away with it?

As Bell presented the plaque for excellence, I thought of how one truly excellent department, science, was under constant pressure from school administrators to *lower* its high standards, "teach to the middle," and keep a nice, traditional grade curve. Did Bell know that Principal Hanley's biggest problem often was not overcrowded classrooms or racial tensions, but interference from bureaucrats in the central administrative office who thought they knew more about running the school than the principal?

I thought of parents who had pressured and intimidated teachers and administrators to get special favors for their kids, to the embarrassment of the children themselves. I thought of colleagues in the auditorium who actually seemed to dislike students, and of a few incompetent teachers who were granted tenure by spineless administrators unwilling to face a fight with lawyers from the teachers' union. I thought of the many *unmet* needs of our students, particularly those of the black seventeen- and eighteen-year-olds who read no better than average fourth graders. They'd "walk"—they'd march up the aisle at graduation to receive their diplomas—but they were totally unprepared to compete afterward for anything but the most menial of jobs. And what of the students with more advantages? Many, including some of the brightest, were bored. Ask them why they were in school and they'd often answer, "It's just a building to come to to meet my friends."

I reflected on the year in progress. Once again, despite the best of intentions, I had failed to make much headway with my two classes of slow-track students. I tried to interest them in literature, but their reading skills were too deficient. No matter what book I gave them, I would hear the same refrain: "it's boring," always a code phrase for "I can't read it." And so I would retreat to having them memorize vocabulary, study grammar, or read newspaper articles aloud. Much as I liked most of these kids, I felt angry and guilty and helpless about the situation. I had been trained to work with students who *could* read. When required to teach ones who couldn't, I felt like a failure. I was angry at a system that pretended that these kids belonged in a twelfth grade classroom. And I was angry at some of my fellow teachers, who successfully maneuvered and politicked to avoid teaching "the dummies."

Fortunately, the bad feelings I had about those two classes of slow and resentful learners were balanced by the pleasure I got from my other three classes of honors students. To remind myself why I still loved teaching after nineteen years, I only had to think of students like Isabel Bigelow, Frankie Nunez, Da-Thanh Nguyen and John Martone. Isabel had it all going for her—brains, beauty, a well-to-do "Boston Brahmin" family. Yet she never let her privileged background show. She was smart but unassuming. Frankie, on the other hand, had grown up on the streets of Brooklyn. He hadn't shed his Puerto Rican accent after moving to Alexandria. But a few weeks after he arrived in my class he was explaining to his classmates the complicated time sequences and personal relationships in William Faulkner's *Light in August*. Da-Thanh, who had only come to America around the time of the fall of Saigon, had more insights into American literature, and wrote better papers, than most of her native-born classmates. And there was John Martone, a favorite of the girls—"the poor woman's Marlon Brando," he was called—

who always took the contrary position in every class discussion as if to match his individualistic style of dress: Japanese one day, Indian shawls another.

I thought to myself, as long as I have the joy of teaching dozens of kids like Isabel, Frankie, Da-Thanh, and John, I can put up with anything, from the frustrations caused by the reading problems of my slow learners to the boredom of listening to speeches by the U.S. Secretary of Education.

In 1959, James B. Conant wrote a much-quoted report, *The American High School Today*. It extolled the big, comprehensive high school "whose programs correspond to the educational needs of all youth in the community." Conant, who issued his pronouncements from the Olympian heights of the presidency of Harvard, argued that a big institution would have something for everybody and that size was a crucial element in a school's success. He reasoned that only a big school could afford to provide a selection of specialized courses broad enough to attract kids with many different interests. It would have something for the budding young scientist and the promising dramatist. It would have vocational education for this kid, Latin for that one. And students could be grouped by ability, so that each was challenged on a proper level.

T. C. Williams *is* such a school. It offers hundreds of courses, from Heating and Air-conditioning Repair to Russian III and Organic Chemistry. Our extra-curricular activities run the gamut, from women's crew and basketball to Frisbee and Ski Club. But we still are not "meeting the educational needs of all youth in the community."

What went wrong with Conant's sensible vision? The answer, I suspect, is that the America Conant wrote about vanished during the quarter of a century since his report was published. It was swept away by demographic, cultural, economic, and technological changes that Conant did not fore-see, and that American high schools (and American families) are only beginning to recognize.

When I came home in the afternoon from Notre Dame High School in Batavia, New York, in the late '50s, I'd prac-tice my jump shot and do my homework. My mother was there, and neighbors kept an eye on me. My television view-ing consisted of the Wednesday-night fights or an occasional Sid Caesar show. I didn't face pressure to try drugs or alcohol. But in the ensuing years, the world I grew up in disappeared. Television and electronic media began to rival and then to far exceed the influence of the classroom teacher. In 1960, parents and teachers were the leading influence on thirteen-to nineteen-year-olds. By 1980, teachers had slipped to fourth place, behind peers, parents, and media (television, ra-dio, and records). By then, a seductive, independent youth culture, with its own music, drugs, precocious sexual mores and values, was challenging the traditional values of school and family. At the same time, as a result of economic pres-sures and the women's movement, mothers of even young children were being drawn out of the home and into the workplace by the millions. Families developed a whole new set of needs that often couldn't be met by traditional high schools.

In some ways, the unchanging routine of high schools pro-vides a sense of reassuring continuity. A high school in the '80s looks and feels pretty much as it did in the '50s. The bell still rings every fifty minutes. The senior prom and the for-tunes of the Titans, our state champion football team, are still staples of school life. Every September, the new senior class officers promise that "this year is going to be different." And the difference usually comes down to the "bigger and better" hotel selected for the senior prom. The motivational posters in the classrooms of earnest teachers say things such as "Today is the first day of the rest of your life" or "You CAN make a difference!" . . . just as they always did.

And yet these familiar images are misleading. In the 1980s, the cheerleaders take the pill, the band does drugs, and the classroom has become peripheral in the lives of many of our "students." Nearly one out of two of them lives with only one natural parent; for the blacks among them, it's closer to two out of three. Jobs and parties take precedence over education. In my day, the "fast" girl was the one who put her hand on the back of your neck during slow dances. Kids are more precocious now. The "college weekend" is now a high school tradition, too, and I've had bright students apologize for turning in papers rendered incoherent by months of steady drug and alcohol abuse.

All these changes have affected the ability of schools and teachers to do their jobs. Members of our experienced science department all attest to a decline in the willingness of the majority of students to do homework on a nightly basis, or put in the consistent effort that science has always required. The science department lately has been viewed as "unreasonably tough," but science teachers insist that they really are demanding less than they were fifteen years ago. The National Assessment of Educational Progress recently reported that only forty-five percent of white students and sixteen percent of black students nationwide can comprehend books used in standard college-preparatory courses.

Some of my students seem to be looking for the same stimulation and entertainment in class that they find in television. As one of them remarked, "Young people have a TV attitude toward school, like it's there to give you a good program and all you have to do is watch, complain, and turn the channel now and then." Kids talk in class, another girl explained to me, the way they talk at home during a TV commercial, ignoring the teacher as if he or she had no more feelings than an electronic image. An angry colleague told her class: "I can't be as interesting as a television program all day long."

At the same time that television, the youth culture, and other social and economic forces were changing the world of young people, schools were experiencing the impact of two momentous occurrences in American society. One was the largest influx of immigrants since the nineteenth century; the other was school desegregation. When Conant wrote his report, the student bodies of most American high schools were fairly homogeneous. But by the 1980s, high schools made up predominantly of a single racial or ethnic group were becoming the exception as a result of busing, the breakdown of old, discriminatory housing patterns and liberal immigration policies. T.C. is typical of thousands of American public schools that are struggling to meet the needs of increasingly diverse student bodies.

This has been a lot for our city and school to digest. Until the late 1950s, Alexandria, Virginia, was still a rather sleepy, segregated Southern community. It had been a thriving center of the slave trade in the early nineteenth century. After the Civil War, "free" blacks settled in black enclaves such as "Cross Canal," "Uptown," and "Mudtown"—the last the site of today's T. C. Williams High School. There was no question where the courthouse derived its power: it was not from "Mudtown," or from the Alfred Street Baptist Church, the local meeting place of the black community, but from the historic old Federal houses that presided in stately elegance over the town's worn brick sidewalks and cobbled streets. Although blacks were able to attend their own publicly financed schools in Alexandria beginning in 1871, they kept to themselves and talked politics in the privacy of Alfred Street.

With the outbreak of World War II, and the rapid expansion of the federal government across the Potomac River, there were changes in Alexandria's population. Well-to-do government officials began settling there. At the same time, there was an influx of poor blacks from rural Georgia and the Carolinas, lured north by a promise of federal jobs and new public housing. In these circumstances, a strong black middle class of the kind that began to emerge across the Potomac in the District of Columbia failed to develop. And the combination of established, well-to-do white families and relatively poor and powerless rural blacks provided the setting for racial tensions and resistance to school desegregation in the '50s and '60s.

The public school system, then headed by the late Superintendent T. C. Williams, at first refused to allow blacks into white schools, but in 1959, under threat of court orders, a few blacks were admitted. The dual system was abandoned only in the mid-1960s, however, and it was not until the early '70s that racial balance was finally achieved.

As if the stresses of desegregation were not enough, Alexandria started to become a haven for refugees from South Korea, Iran, Afghanistan, El Salvador, Nicaragua and other trouble spots. (The "boat people," as everybody calls the local Vietnamese, settled mostly in neighboring Arlington.) Other people came for economic reasons. Between 1980 and 1985 alone, the number of Spanish-speaking children in the Alexandria schools increased by *ninety-six percent*.

In 1985, townhouses costing $200,000 or more looked down from behind high brick walls on the washing put out by poor blacks living in tiny, overcrowded homes. Wealthy white matrons paraded their German Shepherds down the "white" side of Fairfax Street, while young blacks from the Burg public housing projects shot craps on "their" side. T.C. reflected this pluralism. It was a mixture of races, ethnic groups, and economic classes. In the corridors, the sons and daughters of Washington's prominent brushed shoulders with poor blacks, and handsome young Afghan and Hispanic guys necked with blond "redneck" girls.

This diversity is part of T.C.'s appeal. Getting to know "the other half" is one of the educational experiences my school offers. Students and teachers alike feel quietly superior to the predominantly white high schools in the outlying suburbs, where athletic opponents regularly try to provoke our teams by calling white and black players alike "niggers." I get a real thrill when I see an Afghan refugee filling in a white "preppy" on how women have to dress and act in Kabul. We're proud to be a school where blacks and whites attend in almost equal numbers and students come from fifty-five nations and speak twenty-two languages.

But for all the pride we take in our pluralism, diversity presents enormous problems. While the number of blacks attending the Alexandria schools has held steady, white enrollment has declined dramatically, from 12,500 in 1970 (the year before the reorganization to achieve racial balance began) to 3,800 in 1985. The portion of the school population that is white declined from seventy-five percent to thirty-seven percent in that period. Whites still slightly outnumbered blacks at T.C., and, in fact, the black-white balance in the school has been stable since 1980. There's just no more low-income housing available for minorities. Nonetheless, fear of a black "takeover" of the school still infects many of our white staff.

Racial anxieties weren't the only factors in the recent shifts in the school's racial make-up. Trends in real estate and changes in American life styles played a role too. As housing prices rose sharply in the '70s, young families with children tended to settle in more distant, less pricey suburbs, while older families whose children had already graduated from the school system stayed on in houses that were mostly paid for. Meanwhile, new high-rise condominiums, serving mainly childless singles, sprang up in "Condo Canyon." Between 1960 and 1980, the percentage of Alexandria households headed by a single person rose from 12.9 percent to 41.3 percent. And only eighteen percent of the households in Alexandria now have children in the school system, a disturbing omen for the future.

Yet racial factors cannot be completely discounted. When, a few years ago, some children attending the mostly white John Adams Elementary School were ordered bused to Cora Kelly School in the mostly black Lynhaven section, there was an immediate white exodus to private schools. When the busing ended in 1984, an unusually large number of whites suddenly enrolled again in kindergarten classes at John Adams.

Competition from private schools is intense. Fourteen percent of Alexandria's children are enrolled in them. In more affluent sections of town, the figure runs as high as twenty-eight percent. The public school authorities say that the movement of the middle class to private schools has tapered off. Because of the excellent reputation that T. C. Williams has, we're often able to attract kids back to public school after they've finished ninth grade in private schools. But we still feel vulnerable.

This brings me to the significance of all this in terms of the education we are providing at T. C. Williams. Blacks, to be sure, won many victories in Alexandria in the '60s and '70s. Schools were desegregated, a few blacks were appointed to senior administrative positions in the school system, and, in principle, blacks were given access to the same educational facilities as whites. But the whites did not really lose, either. While blacks now make up 41 percent of T.C.'s student body, they do not have 41 percent the power. The school superintendent, the principal, the head of the athletic department, the director of guidance, and eighty-five percent of the teachers are white.

After the early '70s, when the white power structure switched from a policy of foot-dragging to observing the letter of the law, Alexandria shook off its old Southern, segregated image and earned a new one as a progressive-minded community that was committed to desegregation. But providing a school program that satisfied and retained the middle class remained at the top of the power structure's agenda. As living standards rose, so did the educational expectations of the middle-class families that T.C. serves. These people expected to live in better houses, have better jobs, and lead more interesting lives than their parents. And they expected that the schools to which they sent their children would be better too.

T.C. has done its best to satisfy these rising expectations. In truth, T.C. is as elitist as some of the private schools that we teachers resent and make fun of. For the motivated and well-to-do, T.C. is a private school within a public school, a place with advanced courses, lots of electives, good teachers and counselors ready to help with college admissions. Meanwhile, minority students with limited academic skills are channeled into vocational education and promoted whether or not they are progressing academically.

In the 1960s, liberals had a dream: American high schools would bring classes and races closer together. Although the narrow intent of school desegregation was simply to provide blacks with *access* to a decent education, there was also an assumption that blacks would *benefit* from exposure to academically advantaged whites, while whites would gain from the experience of sharing classrooms with blacks. This hope grew out of a deeply held American belief in the public schools as the chief "socializers" in our pluralistic democracy. To make sure that the great gamble on desegregation paid off, the federal government enacted sweeping programs of "compensatory education," such as Head Start and Title I, which were intended to help blacks overcome the academic disadvantages that went with poverty and segregated schools.

But long after desegregation, race is still the great obsession in our school. For years I'd heard white faculty members say ugly things about the behavior and academic performance of black kids, and had undoubtedly let some slip myself. I'd heard white faculty worry aloud that we were on our way to becoming a "black school," or express regret that they hadn't moved to a "whiter" suburb when teaching jobs were more plentiful. I'd heard them worry that the inevitable "black takeover" would come before they retired. I came to realize that these anxieties were mirrored among black faculty members and school officials who had a cynical description of the white majority's policy toward blacks: "Just don't let the niggers burn the building down." They remember the transfers and demotions that accompanied the "gains" of desegregation with considerable bitterness. The Alexandria athletic program was "taken over by white rednecks," a black coach complained. "They used our great black athletes to build names for themselves, but they didn't give a damn about those kids." After desegregation, black teachers from the formerly all-black high school found themselves teaching junior high, and black coaches were assigned to junior varsity teams. The anger of the black staff is double-edged. Many feel badly treated by a school system that is still controlled by whites, and they feel that black students often are poorly served by this same system.

Five months before Bell's visit, when the 1983–84 school year was just beginning, the "education crisis" still seemed remote from my daily routine. I was too busy grading papers or taking my turn at the Xerox machine to spend long hours contemplating the future of the American high school. Although I had friends all over the school, I was more isolated in my classroom than I realized. I concentrated on the things I thought I *could* affect, such as improving my students' writing and getting them interested in literature.

This book is the result of my own education, or reeducation, about high school. During the two-and-one-half years I worked on it, I came to realize how little I'd known about the place I'd spent most of my professional life. I was told that the chubby white girl I was sure had never had a date actually had had a series of affairs. I found out that the student with the permanent smile on her face saw a psychiatrist three times a week. Some of the guys in my honors English course always looked tired. I thought it was just senior slump. Then I discovered that they were "on the boat"—the drug love boat, which they had purchased on some of the most dangerous streets in Washington, D.C. Such were my "innocent" students.

High school, I began to see, was a sideshow for a lot of my students, a place to meet friends and kill some time before getting on with the "real" life of after-school jobs, a "mature" romantic relationship, weekend parties, television and the video scene. The kid with the highest scholastic aptitude test score in the school confided that he was "bored."

As I poked and pried into unfamiliar corners of the school, I also became more keenly aware of the tensions and political crosscurrents swirling around and in it: the friction between administrators and parents; the conflicts between the central administrative office and individual schools; and, of course, the ever-present tensions of race.

As I went about my research, I was forced to think hard about my institution. What could be done better? Could anything be done to improve the poor performance of disadvantaged kids? How could high school, which had changed so little since horse-and-buggy days, be updated to serve students and families in the Information Age? How could school be made more exciting, interesting, and useful for students? And how could it do a better job of supporting the hard-pressed American family of the '80s?

One can be envious of the '80s kids. In many ways, they have it better than their parents and teachers did. The obligation of military service ceased with the end of the peacetime draft in 1973. Today, with a minimum of hassles, a young person reaching maturity can smoke marijuana, get an abortion, obtain birth control, flick on any amount of electronic gadgetry, and (especially if white and middle class) get a job that will pay for these comforts and pleasures. A kid can slide through high school and still get into some college that's desperate to keep up its admissions.

Yet these kids need more, not less, from schools. In a world of information overload, they need more help in separating the important and significant from the trivial and merely entertaining. We needed information from schools. Kids growing up in the '80s need to learn how to filter, interpret, and understand the flood of information. In a society in which divorce is commonplace and the youth culture puts a premium on precocious sex, heavy drinking and drug use, children need more emotional support and guidance than ever. In a time in our history when much is given but little is asked, they need real challenges against which they can shape their character, values, and minds.

I agree with Prof. Ken Macrorie of Western Michigan University, who says that one of our great blind spots in schooling is that "when we walk into classrooms we forget that we are still human beings." Sometimes I'll see in a flash, usually by accident, how much students look to teachers for counseling and recognition. They look to us for help in getting over a personal crisis. They look for opportunities to display their unique talents. They look for chances to help others. They look for intellectual stimulation.

Scattered through the pages that follow are one teacher's ideas about how to make high school really count for kids. In theory, of course, schools already do this. In practice, the jobs of teachers, the security of well-paid school bureaucrats and the schools' all-important "image" come first. Defending the status quo has become an end in itself. The prevailing attitude of teachers and school bureaucrats is, "We're fine—don't rock the boat." This may have been a prudent philosophy in the past. But it is one that schools can ill afford now, when they are being overwhelmed by new forces, and everyone—the poor and the affluent alike—is questioning their effectiveness.

2

Tales Out of School (I)

At a benefit for a local theater group, a woman in a dressed-for-success suit comes up to me. "Are you with the World Bank?" she asks, looking me up and down. I'm wearing my only suit that isn't speckled with red ink stains from correcting English essays.

"No, I teach English at T. C. Williams High School."

I can feel an immediate strain on the conversation.

"You don't meet many *high school* teachers," she says, feigning interest. "How long have you been doing *that*?"

"Thirteen years."

She looks puzzled, as if she's thinking, What's wrong with this guy—can't he find decent work? But what I want to say to this woman, this assistant to some deputy chief assistant in some corner of the federal government, is: "Lady, I bet my job is more exciting than yours *any day*!"

My love affair with teaching began the day in the fall of 1966 when I stood in front of my first class. I was a graduate student at Loyola University in Chicago and had been assigned to teach freshman composition. For all my anxiety about this assignment, I could have been lecturing to a roomful of Nobel laureates. For weeks before that first class, I'd had a nightmare about freezing up. Suddenly I would have absolutely nothing to say. In my waking hours I worried that I didn't know enough to be a teacher and needed more time to study.

When the big moment finally came, I was sweating so hard

my glasses got steamy. My attack of nerves wasn't helped by the class's makeup: twenty-one women and only three men. "This guy will be a pushover," I heard a girl mutter as I walked in. The first fifteen minutes were a haze as I quickly outlined the course. Then I began to relax. I began to be myself. By the end of the hour I was having fun!

Since then, I've probably taught 15,000 classes, but I think in that first hour I experienced most of the positive feelings that were to keep me in teaching. I'd be less than honest if I didn't admit that I enjoyed having a captive audience (which almost always included attractive and interesting young women). I also felt the first intimations of my own burning determination to have *my* students do well. Call it pride. Call it competitive spirit. I knew I wanted to "reach" these students in some way. I wanted and needed the recognition that comes from doing an exceptional job of preparing kids. Many years later, I still feel great satisfaction when the school system publishes the results of national "advanced placement" tests and the high scores of my students stand out.

But there was more behind my early enthusiasm for teaching than ego gratification or pride. I felt I could make a difference, could affect my students' lives by adding some small bit of insight. And that made me feel important. Years later, I read Arthur Miller's introduction to his collected plays. In explaining the theme of *Death of a Salesman*, Miller wrote that man's greatest need—"a need greater than hunger or sex or thirst"—is "to leave a thumbprint somewhere on the world."

That says it, I thought to myself. That's why I teach.

Where that need came from is a complicated question. I think it was put there in some mysterious way by my father and mother, by the priests and nuns who were my own teachers and by an irreverent college English professor by the name of Victor Commerchero.

My mother and her father taught me to love literature and poetry. My grandfather was a concocter of poems—not epics by any means, but poems that got his grandchildren interested in the fun and flow of words. I'll never forget his most ambitious effort, about an Italian barber who stole $5 from the collection basket at Sunday mass at St. Joseph's Church. Every year I start my students off with about nine weeks of poetry; I feel it's at the heart of literature, and I like teaching it more than anything else. Teaching poetry now, I get the same emotional "peak" I did reading poems as a boy.

Through poetry, I've always felt, the kids can see my emotions, get to know and feel comfortable with me. It's my secret way of breaking the ice with each new class. In a week we can cover ten or twenty poems with the widest range of ideas and feelings. We can study the classical one day— something like Shakespeare's "Let me not to the marriage of true minds"—and the modern and outrageous the next. I like Judith Grahn's "The Marilyn Monroe Poem," in which the speaker digs up Monroe's bones and goes forth to beat leering men to death with them. That *really* breaks the ice. But if it weren't for my grandfather's crazy poems, I'd probably be starting the year off with grammar.

My father played a different but no less important role in pointing me toward my profession. His dad had emigrated from Ireland and had wanted *him* to be a teacher—a "professor," as all teachers were called back in County Mayo. Instead, he became a doctor in the western New York village of Le Roy. After many a blizzard, his car followed the plow down back-country roads on the way to visit sick patients in their homes. He taught me that serving people is the highest calling and showed me that if you have a passion for your work, you are on your way to a happy life. At 79, he still makes house calls.

Meanwhile, the priests and nuns at the church schools I attended were having their effect. A whole generation of Catholic boys remember Sister Carmelita, whose left hook and deep love for her students left their mark on all of us. Those teacher-nuns and teacher-priests were esteemed in our community. They instilled an appreciation of hard work and excellence. We knew that the priests who taught us could read Latin and Greek and seemed better educated than the teachers in public schools. And they never ceased to let us know that we were getting a better education than what they disparagingly called "the publics." Inevitably, I began to picture myself in the role of the respected clergy who were teaching me: people like Father Prina and Father Rutecki, who seemed to love their work and their lives and were fussed over at dinner by my mother and provided with free medical care by my father.

Nowadays I often feel ambivalent about the Catholic world in which I grew up. For years I wouldn't teach Joyce's *Portrait of the Artist*, so accurate and painful to me was the picture of Irish Catholic boyhood and the conflict over entering the priesthood. I've never told my students that I spent three years in a Jesuit seminary after high school, or that I realized my flesh was weaker than my spirit the day a beautiful Italian girl came to visit her seminarian cousin and her long, dark hair somehow brushed against my face as I sat next to her in my priestly robes. But I guess there's still some priest in me. Not long ago a mother wrote me a note of thanks for "shepherding" her daughters through school. I hope she doesn't think I'm some damned priest, I thought. But try as I have to deny it, there's still a part of me that just substituted literature for religion and my students for my "flock."

For a while after the seminary I forgot about being a teacher. I was still trying to please my father and thought that becoming a doctor might be the next best thing to being a Jesuit priest. Then along came Victor Commerchero, an irreverent Californian who taught me English at Canisius College in Buffalo. After three years of piety and repression at the seminary, Victor's cynicism was refreshing. He grated on the Jesuits, who ran Canisius, probably because he was a better teacher than most of the priests. But I took to him right away. He was one of the first lay teachers I had had—a guy who wasn't religious but was a great teacher. The year I met him, I stopped going to church regularly, maybe because he made me feel that literature could provide as good a means as religion for exploring values.

Victor had no qualms about denigrating great poets and playwrights if their work struck him as sentimental nonsense. He had it in for Tennyson. But he made me see in Hamlet my own tendency toward indecision. Victor became a role model, partly because he communicated something of the world beyond Canisius and Buffalo at a time when I already was preparing myself to get out, but also because he made me feel that I could be true to myself and still teach. I could teach, in other words, without wearing a priestly black "dress."

In 1974, I came to a crossroads. I had moved to the Washington area and was teaching at T. C. Williams, but also studying law at night. When I passed the bar exam that year, I realized I had to choose. Fortunately, I was beginning to understand myself a little better. I knew why I'd wanted that degree, and it had very little to do with any desire to become a lawyer. I had wanted to prove something to myself. In a society that has a low opinion of the teaching profession—especially of the men who enter it—I wanted to show that I could be "more than a teacher." But once I'd proved that, I could let go of it. I could do what I wanted to do, which was to teach.

No matter how long I teach, I still get opening day jitters. As I walk into my first class, the faces are all unfamiliar. These aren't "my" kids, I think to myself. "My" kids are at Michigan State, Syracuse, the University of Virginia, or wherever last year's class ended up. I catch myself thinking, You'll never take the place of Sarah Berg, Juan Conde, Sharon Wellington, Ben Moerman, and those other great kids from last year.

The first thing I realize is that five students are standing in the back of the room with no desks. The custodians and the guidance department, which assigns students to classrooms, have again neglected to get together on that minor detail. I rush to another room and beg another teacher for the needed desks. Back in my own class I get everybody settled, take roll, pass out a vocabulary list, and read a poem, "Advice to My Son," by J. Peter Meinke. It's hardly a classic, but I hope it will break the ice. At the same time I'm thinking to myself, How can anybody, let alone a bunch of half-awake seventeen-year-olds, get into poetry at eight-thirty in the morning?

Then I feel the old familiar anxiety I have at the start of each new year. Will my passion for teaching have mysteriously disappeared? Am I too old—too distant in age and experience from these students, who seem younger every year? Do I still have it? Can I turn them on to literature? Can I bring this mixed bunch together?

As I'm worrying, a girl raises her hand and comments on Meinke's use of bread and wine imagery; the field-goal kicker on the football team follows up; the president of the senior class moves on to the flower imagery, ties it to the bread and wine symbols, and cuts through to the heart of the poem. Hands are going up all over the place, and suddenly I feel it. It's coming back. I'm not too old. This should be another great year.

Teachers have an old saying: "To get students interested, you have to go in their door, but take them out yours." To me this means that I have to start with literature kids like and can relate to. From years of teaching, I've found that their two main areas of concern are parents and sex. So, early in the school year, I introduce them to poetry through works that deal with those two obsessions. Most of them like Lawrence Ferlinghetti's "In the Pennycandy Store Beyond the El," about a boy's first consciousness of a girl's "breathless breasts." Even the difficult, metaphysical works of John Donne seem to appeal to them when they deal with some kind of romantic relationship.

This is what I'm thinking in the fourth week of school as I play a record of Richard Burton reading Donne's "The Good Morrow" to one of my advanced senior English classes.

> My face in thine eye, thine in mine appeares
> And true plaine hearts do in the faces rest,
> Where can we finde two better hemispheares
> Without sharpe North, without declining West?

It's my favorite love poem, and as I hear Burton reading these lines I'm thinking of my wife and the world she's created for me with our children. I'm close to tears.

All of a sudden three boys in the front of the class are laughing. I've got a short fuse to begin with—an "Irish temper"—and I'd been up twice the night before with Claire, our youngest, and am going on four hours' sleep. I explode. "You guys can get your asses out of here for good if you think it's such a joke."

We listen to two more Donne poems and start a discussion, but the class is ruined. Why did I lose my cool? I wonder afterward. These are nice boys—bright, witty, full of life—and for all I know, they were laughing at something funny. Besides, didn't I hate poetry at their age? But then I think, Hey, I *should* have screamed at them. Why should they be messing around when they have a chance to experience some of the greatest poetry in the English language?

Forget it, I think. Lose them today, come back and get them tomorrow.

The longer I teach, the more I realize the importance of "staying loose." The rigid, programmed class leaves no room for wonder, feeling, emotion. The books on pedagogy stress the importance of control in the classroom. But it's often when things are a little out of control—when I get a queasy feeling in my stomach—that real learning takes place.

For years, when I would teach a novel I controlled what passages were read out loud in class. Not long ago, I let kids in my advanced literature class read and comment on *their* favorite passages. One day, Jeanne Berger, a sweet, innocent-looking girl in my seventh-period class chooses the most sexually explicit passage in William Faulkner's *Light in August*. This is when the main character, Joe Christmas, sleeps with a woman for the first time. The passage is Faulkner at his best, but I'd often shied away from it, worrying about what the kids would think. Jeanne gives it a wonderful reading, bringing out all the beauty and pathos of the scene in a way I never could. I think to myself, How horribly we teachers underestimate kids.

Staying loose also gives luck a chance to work its way. Some of my best "pedagogical moves" come by pure chance—at times by default. One day I walk into my sixth-period class intending to pass out copies of *Henry IV, Part I*.

Panic! It suddenly hits me that all the copies are with my two other advanced classes. I glance desperately at the book shelf and pull down thirty copies of Toni Morrison's novel about a black family, *Song of Solomon*. The all-white class goes wild. "Best thing we've read all year." "Why don't we read more like it?" I had been into the heavies—Shakespeare, Faulkner, Hardy, Joyce. But because we had run out of *Henry IV*, all my advanced classes now read Morrison's novel.

The scene is the John F. Kennedy Center for the Performing Arts in Washington, where I've bused some of my English students for an uplifting evening of culture. The play is to be *American Buffalo*, starring Al Pacino. Waiting for the curtain to go up, the T. C. Williams contingent makes a heartwarming picture: a cultural outing with the English teacher. I look around with satisfaction at these bright, vivacious teen-agers, many of them neat, well-combed 17-year-old girls. Then on comes Pacino, in the role of a small-time New York hoodlum. "Mother f——," "c——t," "mother f——." I'm stunned, squirming, afraid to look left or right at the "innocents" who had been entrusted to their English teacher's care that evening—or at the mother who has come along and was sitting five seats away. But afterward I relax. It appears I was the only one shocked. And the "young innocents" seemed to enjoy demonstrating their worldly sophistication for their anxious teacher's benefit.

A Korean boy who's been in this country for only two months approaches my desk. He's nodding, almost bowing deferentially. "Mr. Welsh," he stammers, "I want more words."

At first I don't understand. "Ten a night not enough," he says.

"Okay, sure, but are you certain you can manage more?"

"Yes, sir," he says, trying to suppress a look of disdain. He reaches in his school bag and comes up with a tape recorder.

"I want you to read words for me each day."

So every day for a week I dutifully pronounce twenty new words into his tape recorder. At the end of the week, he's bowing in front of my desk again.

"Mr. Welsh, you not give me enough words. I need forty a night."

The semester goes on; the pampered preppies struggle with (and complain about) ten words a night in their native language; the Korean boy waits each day after school with his tape recorder for the next forty.

"Robert" is a young black male in my slow-track class. In basketball, his turnaround jump shot is one of the best in the Washington area, but reading a paragraph out loud leaves him as breathless as a five-minute overtime.

The class has an international complexion. Along with local black kids, it's full of recent arrivals from faraway places who need work on their English: Koreans, Taiwanese and Pakistanis, among others. "Robert" calls all of them the same: "motherf—— Puerto Ricans."

I am determined to improve his understanding of world geography, as well as his reading, and one day I bring in a big world map and ask the foreign students to identify their countries. One by one they stride briskly to the map and point out their homelands. "Robert" shows an interest and finally says, "Hey, Welsh, let me show 'em where I live."

He goes to the map, pauses, and starts searching. His finger glides over Europe, Africa, and South America and finally comes to rest on Australia. "Here it is," he shouts. "D.C.— chocolate city!"

The foreign kids are all chuckling. Suddenly a Taiwanese rushes to the map and puts his finger just south of Washington, the exact location of Alexandria, and blurts out, "You here, man, you from here."

A mother concerned by her daughter's grade, a C, is calling. She is, I would say, a member of Alexandria's elite. The family is affluent, and her husband has a good job with the government. On her occasional visits to school, she's fashionably dressed.

The conversation starts off pleasantly enough, with her telling me she had read in college some of the same poetry her daughter is studying now. She mentions the name of a very prestigious New England private liberal arts institution.

"Where did *you* go to college?" she inquires.

"Canisius."

"Where's *that*?"

I sense that the game is on. Her daughter is teetering between a C and a B in my English class, and this mother is worried that a C could tip the scales against her daughter's acceptance at her old alma mater.

"How do you grade?"

I start to explain, but she cuts in. She really thought some of her daughter's essays deserved B's, not the C's they got. I say that her daughter is certainly capable of A's, but hasn't been putting enough effort into her writing. We arrange to meet with the daughter the next day.

The moment they walk in I notice that there is something askew. The mother is dressed as if she's just stepped out of the pages of *Town and Country* magazine. She's smiling and talkative. The daughter looks as if she's just driven a tractor-trailer rig cross-country. She's wearing old jeans and a tattered shirt and is silent during most of the conference. As we talk, I feel that the mother is employing charm, intimidation and a subtle kind of class warfare—the poor teacher vs. the woman of status. The daughter just sits, passive and sullen.

Two days later the girl takes my quarterly exam. When the period ends she hands in a single sheet of paper, blank except for her name. I'm flabbergasted, but the daughter explains.

"My mother had no right putting on that show the other day," she says. "This is none of her business."

Lunch duty in the school cafeteria. I'm guarding line three to make sure nobody cuts in or tries to make off with one of today's specials ("teen-teasers" and "surfburgers"). It's noisy; it's crowded; it's occasionally tense. The cafeteria is the only place except the auditorium where everybody comes together, the Harvard bound and the Phase 1 kids (those reading at the level of sixth graders or below), the jocks and the eggheads, foreign kids and native born.

I'm standing next to the class valedictorian, discussing a few sentences in the essays she's submitting to Harvard with her early-admissions application. I'm thinking how unpredictable the admissions departments of Ivy League schools are. They'd be crazy not to take this young woman, with her 1500-plus SATs, straight A's, perfect scores on seven advanced placement tests, a position as co-captain of T.C.'s national championship crew, and a pleasing, unpretentious personality to boot.

Suddenly there's trouble in the line up ahead. Twenty Afghan students, joking and laughing in a big circle, are joined by two Afghan girls. A black girl with an athletic build, in line to the rear, moves in and demands that the newcomers go to the end of the queue. "My friends are staying," says one of the Afghan girls in a British accent.

The black girl goes into an Ali shuffle, but the Afghan, half her size, responds with an obviously expert kung fu stance. No wonder the Russians are having trouble, I think, as I rush to get between them. "Now ladies," I tell them as the black girl tries to leap over my shoulder at her adversary. I mediate a settlement that's more expedient than just: the Afghan can stay and the American girl can go to the front of the line to buy her surfburger. Peace reigns. Now back to Harvard applications.

"Hey! Take off that Walkman and give it to me until class is over," I shout at Roy, a long-haired, mustached white senior.

A scowl. A look of indignation. "Hay is for horses, man. I ain't no horse. Show me some respect and I'll show you some."

"Would you please give me your Walkman until class is over."

"I'll put it in my bookbag, but I ain't givin' it to you."

"All right. Put it in the bag."

Five minutes later, the sound of rock music wafts from the bag, distracting me from a discussion of action verbs and linking verbs.

"Give me that bag!"

"That's my personal property. You can't touch it!"

"Okay, go to the assistant principal's office. I'll be there at the end of class."

The ruined class ends and the next group comes pouring in. The kids are delightful and bright. We discuss last night's reading, *Light in August*, my favorite novel. I forget about the kid with the Walkman cooling his heels in the assistant principal's office. Later in the day I catch up with the assistant principal. He's made the kid stay after school.

A few weeks later, I get a request for a report on the guy, who is a prominent member of the school's "redneck" clique. The assistant principal is getting ready to kick him out of school. The guy's driving all the teachers crazy, missing classes, disrupting lessons, coming to school stoned. I happen to talk to his guidance counselor, who casually informs me that the guy was an abused child, hasn't seen his father in years, was just kicked out of his home by his mother, and is living alone in an apartment, working at a full-time job after school.

"He's doing okay in class," I tell the assistant principal. "Let's give him one more shot." He continues to give us problems for the rest of the year but finally graduates. Was he worth the lost instruction time, the frustration, the waste of emotional energy? Should I have pushed to get rid of him? I don't know. I really don't.

The poem is "Lunch on Omaha Beach," by Bink Noll. The class is discussing how the neat rows of crosses on Omaha Beach in Normandy cover up the chaos, disorder, and horror of war—what Noll calls the "beast who naked wakes in us and walks/In flags." I'm wondering, as I often do in class, Does this mean anything to these kids? It's the day before the big homecoming game and dance, and I imagine students' minds are on dates and parties.

The discussion digresses from Omaha Beach and begins to focus on the new, controversial Vietnam memorial on the Mall in Washington, a stark monument consisting of a long, low stone wall on which are inscribed the names of every American fatality. I'm recalling a social studies teacher telling me how the war is of little interest to students today. I ask how many kids have been to see the new memorial, and a few hands go up.

"My father's name is on it," says Colleen Kelly in the front row.

The class falls silent. Maybe five seconds pass. I feel choked up. It crosses my mind that two seats behind Colleen sits Minh Vu, a Vietnamese girl who escaped with her dad as Saigon was falling. I want to say something to Colleen, ask her about her dad, but I'm afraid to. I always want literature to "relate to life," to be something the kids can feel in their guts. But this time it's too close. I look at the clock. Only four mintues left. I move on, trying to discuss the last stanza of the poem.

It's the time of year when members of the new senior class come to have their pictures taken for their yearbook. I'm a little surprised to see a guy I recognize as a dropout standing in the line outside the conference room where the photographer is charging as much as $180 for a packet of pictures. A somewhat emaciated, sleepy individual, this young man had been in my class for about half the previous year until he dropped out of school. By then he had a drug habit and a criminal record. What surprises me even more is that he is holding a tiny baby in his arms.

"What's the baby's name?" I ask, deducing that he is a new father. What's going on in my mind is that I want to act as if it were a perfectly normal situation. At least, I rationalize, he's admitting the baby is his and seems to be caring for it, not like so many of the other teen-age fathers I've taught who deny or joke about the children they've created and who never show up for our class for prospective parents. But part of me wants to scream. What chance does this child have? The father is just seventeen and semiliterate. Already he's had brushes with the law. But I say, "Good to see you," and move on to class.

Some time ago, my wife, five months pregnant, was in the hospital with premature labor pains. I was out of school for a couple of days, and the first day back I was greeted by a cherubic-faced seventeen-year-old senior. She consoled her concerned-looking forty-year-old English teacher: "Mr. Welsh, don't worry about those premature contractions. I had those with my second child and everything turned out fine."

One night I'm grading composition papers at home, finding out what my students have to say about W. H. Auden's poem "As I Walked Out One Evening." My children are sleeping and the papers are spread out on the dining room table. There's the usual mix of the horrible, the mediocre, and the excellent. Suddenly, I'm riveted. I can hardly believe that a seventeen-year-old could write with such penetrating clarity. I look at the name: Elisabeth Orshansky. As the semester proceeds, Elisabeth keeps coming up with papers that I marvel at.

She becomes my teacher, providing new insights into poems and novels that I'd been teaching for more than ten years. But when I try to probe discreetly for the secret of this brilliance, I run into a dead end. I know her parents emigrated from Russia in the '50s. Perhaps she grew up in a strict family situation away from the American video culture. No, she assures me, her upbringing was typical. She "watched television a lot." Did her parents read to her a great deal when she was young? "No, they just had lots of books around and I guess I just followed their example."

A postcard arrives unexpectedly from Mark Lange, a student of mine five years ago. Mark is writing to say he's just finished Dartmouth and is cycling through Europe. He just wants to let me know that a poem we'd done in class five years ago had inspired him during his travels. It was James Dickey's "Cherrylog Road," about a wild young man on his motorcycle. Mark even quotes the concluding lines: "Wringing the handle bars for speed/Wild to be wreckage forever."

Some of them do remember, I think to myself.

It's the last class of the day, and we're rolling. Suddenly there's an annoying knock on the door. I open it and find a tall, attractive black woman standing there. She looks too young to be someone's mother. "Can I help you?" I ask, trying to conceal my irritation at the interruption.

Then it hits me. It's Lettie Moses, Class of '78—but she's taller and slimmer than I'd remembered. She's graduated from Smith College and is on her way to the University of Michigan Law School. Lettie, from the Alexandria housing projects. Lettie, whose loving mother and father were determined to see her succeed.

"I just dropped by to say hello," she says.

We talk in the hall for a few minutes, catching up on four years of news. Her visit makes my day. I think what she really was saying to me was "I just wanted to let you know I made it." And I was thinking, Lettie, I know you would have made it without me, but just being a tiny part of your growth and success, just witnessing it, that's what teaching is all about.

3

Families

"How do you spell 'vasectomy'?" asks a girl after school.

"Just like it sounds, I think. Why do you want to know?"

"I'm writing to a friend about my father's."

"Oh," I say, feeling a little nonplussed. "Did he decide he doesn't want any more children?"

"No, he's having his *reversed*. He just remarried and decided he needed another kid to fulfill his life."

With that she launches into a hilarious monologue about her dad, her mom, the new wife. Joan Rivers would have had trouble keeping up with this kid's wit. Gradually, though, the pain surfaces.

"I guess I'm doing okay now, but for a while I was really screwed up." She goes on to tell me how her grades took a tailspin after her parents divorced in the middle of ninth grade.

"You're lucky," I say. "Some kids never seem to recover from a divorce and just go on messing up their lives to get back at their parents."

"You know," she says, "once I accepted the divorce and realized I couldn't change things, I was able to see how comical it all is—the thought of my father going through the two a.m. feedings and the diapers bit again."

As she's leaving the room I can't help asking if she hopes her father's operation works.

"If he'd gotten it reversed before, probably not. It's really strange that all this is happening when I'm wondering my-

34

self what it would be like to have kids. But now I guess a baby brother would be kind of nice."

Conversations like that remind me how much growing up has changed since I was a teen-ager. I always want to believe that my innocent-looking students are living the same relatively sheltered life I did back when divorce was a rarity, coffee was a "drug," French kissing was considered cause for hell's fires, and the nuns policing our school dances threw towels over the exposed shoulders of girls in evening gowns.

"Due to the rising divorce rate of the past thirty years, I find that I am rapidly becoming a minority," wrote twelfth-grader Matt Elmore. "My family is still a family. My parents are still married. They have owned and lived in the same house for twenty-five years, on Maple Street, U.S.A. When I call a girl on the phone I must know beforehand whether she'll be at her mother's house or her father's apartment. When I tell my mother that Bob's parents are divorcing, she just sighs a little. In another era a similar situation could have caused great anguish and Bob's parents would have been the talk of the neighborhood. Today they're just another statistic. 'What's to become of the children?' is a question that is rarely asked anymore. Divorce trauma, like the cold, is far too common to be taken seriously."

Matt concluded his essay with a poignant comment about his peers: "I'm lucky my parents have stayed together. Unlike so many of my friends, I've never had to cry on a holiday."

You might say that we're witnessing the coming of age of the "latchkey generation"—the kids who've spent most of their lives letting themselves into empty homes after school. These teen-agers have lived through a divorce epidemic, economic pressures that caused millions of mothers to move from the home to the workplace, and a decade of social turmoil. It's hardly surprising that their attitudes and behavior have been shaped by that experience.

Guidance counselors tell me that the family dinner, at which generations once routinely came together and shared experiences, seems to be a disappearing ritual among the families we serve. Their information suggests that many kids now get their own dinners, or go out and buy them at the local fast food restaurant. A divorced father who returns home after 8 o'clock from a high-pressure Washington job was asked by a counselor how his son gets dinner. "I expect him to get it for *me*," he replied.

By the time kids reach their teens, they're beginning to be drawn into a youth culture that competes with schools and families for their time and attention. Huck Finn would rub his eyes in disbelief at the lives of fourteen-year-olds these days. Huck never sneaked out of school to watch rock video on TV, take drugs or engage in casual sex in the homes of fathers and mothers who (in the case of our clientele) are often off saving the country and the world at the Pentagon, Capitol Hill, or other Washington power centers.

We have thirteen-year-old kids who drink heavily at parties and throw up in the bushes in some of Alexandria's most prestigious neighborhoods. Older kids often party through the weekend at houses from which parents seem to have disappeared. Alcohol flows, drugs are routinely available and there are plenty of empty beds upstairs.

As of June 1985, 115 of T.C.'s 1,200 girls (and another 22 in the two junior highs) had become pregnant since the previous September, according to the count of School Nurse Marianne Heil. And this figure included only girls who used public health services and decided to have the babies. Four prospective mothers had just turned thirteen. Then there was the T.C. girl who got pregnant in April 1984, had an abortion in June, got pregnant again in August, had an abortion in September, became pregnant again in November, and had another abortion in December. One particularly active young male, nicknamed the "baby doctor" by classmates, was reported to have impregnated five girls at three different schools, including three at T. C. Williams, all of whom were carrying a child of his at the same time.

Joan Myers, who teaches the Family Life (sex ed) course at George Washington Junior High School, describes the fourteen- and fifteen-year-olds she encounters as "jaded" and "sophisticated in a pseudo-worldly way." Myers says their conversations often sound like those of her thirty-year-old friends. "I'm sick of guys and I think I'll stop having sex for a while," Myers heard one girl say. She was fifteen. "I've seen girls you'd want to have as your daughter in here debating among themselves the advantages of oral sex," Heil told me. "The message is, 'It's okay, Prince does it'," said a senior.

Venereal disease is a real problem. "It's standing room only in the local VD clinics," said Heil halfway through the '84–85 school year. The middle-class mother of a fourteen-year-old girl was in tears when she confided to a friend that her daughter was suffering from VD. "I know she has too much freedom, but I can't give up my social life to watch her all the time," she said.

The big "scandal" in the fall of '84 took place at a party held at the house of a student. When the parents returned home, they found the daughter of an affluent neighbor in *their* bed with a member of the football team.

A player I knew well on one of our teams told me confidentially that several members of the starting lineup got "up" for games by snorting cocaine in the school parking lot. Nobody ever knew, and, after all, they do it in the pros.

The changes in the way kids are growing up have placed tremendous new pressures on those of us who work in schools.

Schools have always had a function beyond just educating the minds of students. Building character and reinforcing values taught at home—values such as honesty, diligence, and concern for others—have long been part of a good school's mandate. But school people assumed that the family had the main responsibility. That isn't so clear anymore. A lot of parents want and need much more from schools now than just good test scores for their kids. They're looking to schools to do more of the jobs parents traditionally have done.

Our record on responding to this expectation has been mixed.

T.C.'s guidance department is really a Band-Aid operation. Not counting the school psychologist and social worker, there are only eight full-time guidance counselors, one for every 270 students, hardly enough to provide much individual attention or follow-up. Kids are always complaining that they come to counselors with a problem that seems immense but get only a "quick answer." Our youngest counselor is thirty-nine. And not all the counselors have the training or temperament for dealing with the complex emotional crises that kids bring to them.

Guidance and the teaching faculty often seem to live in separate worlds, not sharing helpful information about the lives or problems of individual students. The emotional side of kids is "assigned" to guidance counselors while their intellectual development is the responsibility of teachers. Tensions between counselors and teachers are notorious. Teachers blame the guidance department for sending them too many students, or academically unsuitable ones. We imagine counselors sitting in their offices, chatting with individual students while we control and entertain a crowd of twenty or more kids at a time. Privately, we worry that the counselors are collecting information about us from talkative students.

However, T.C. now does more parenting on behalf of families than would have been imaginable a few decades ago. Around Alexandria, if there's a kid to be gotten into college, or a parent who's having trouble controlling a child, the word is, "See Jim." Jim is James McClure, a graying, fortyish former music teacher who heads the guidance department. Guidance is responsible for college admissions, testing, class assignments and scores of other things, such as filling out referral forms for "homebounds"—pregnant girls and others authorized to have a tutor come to their apartment or house. But a growing part of its work now is advising families in crisis.

"We do a lot of mopping up here," says Jim, a man with an unusual gift for combining honesty with parents about their children with a compassion that seems to say, I realize it isn't easy. "I see too many parents who want a quick fix for their kids. Parents are tired. It's the fast society we live in. Young people are crying out for help. It's an across-the-board phenomenon, from the wealthiest to the poorest. So many people who are the picture of confidence and success in their careers are desperate when it comes to their own children. These parents will call the school, at their wit's end, and say, 'I know you can't do anything, but.' And after the 'but' comes the hope that we *will* do something. What it really comes down to is that a growing number of parents expect the schools, especially the guidance counselors, to do their parenting."

I often duck into the guidance office for a cup of coffee before my first class. Sometimes I have to weave through throngs of kids and parents. Counselor Jimmi Barnwell is meeting with a father and daughter. The father is divorced and not married. The girl has resided with him since her mother went to live with a boyfriend. Lately the girl's been playing hooky—leaving home to "catch the bus," then sneaking back to watch the soaps and pretending to be the housekeeper when the school calls. The session is interrupted by a phone call from a mother who hasn't seen her daughter in several days. Could Barnwell find out if the girl has been attending class without making it seem as if she was "checking up on her"? After Barnwell hangs up, the meeting with the father and daughter resumes. So goes a typical morning in the guidance office.

With a five-year-old son, three-year-old daughter, and fourteen-year-old stepdaughter, I'm sympathetic to the pressures that families face in the '80s. But I'd be dishonest if I didn't say that, as a teacher, I'm tired of the schools getting all the blame. If parents have legitimate complaints about the quality of help they're getting from the school, we have real concerns about the quality of parenting our students receive.

A lot of couples seem to have slid into parenthood without thinking deeply about the qualities and commitment required to raise stable, independent, happy children. Having a fancy degree or being a "pillar of the community" is no guarantee of success. We've had children of school board members with drug problems. Great kids come from homes where parents are divorced, as well as from "stable" homes; from poor families as well as rich ones. In fact, it's the values of middle-class families with plenty of advantages that I often find myself questioning.

They've tried so hard, and so successfully, to control their lives, their careers, their mortgage payments, and their employees that some of them begin believing they can "manage" their kids too. Their children become just another badge of material success. I suspect, in fact, that a lot of the youthful behavior that worries us—the drinking, sex, drugs, and low motivation—is really a rebellion against parental attitudes that seem to value a kid's achievement more than his or her worth as a person.

My students always get stirred up when we read "Why Youth Is in Revolt," an essay by Bruno Bettelheim. Bettelheim writes about the pressures that parents put on young people:

> The modern, middle-class family still feels that its justification has to be derived from what it produces, but the only thing it produces now are children. Their perfection should justify the labors, if not the very existence of the family . . . Perhaps we were all better off when children were seen as a gift of God, however they turned out, and not something the high quality of which provides justification of our family.

There's so much interest in what Bettelheim has to say that we seldom get around to discussing the essay's organization, tone, and language before kids start volunteering that Bettelheim is right on the mark and giving examples from their own lives.

"No matter what I do, it seems they aren't satisfied," says a student who has 1400-plus SAT scores, is a skilled athlete, and has just gained early admission into one of the country's most competitive colleges. "If I bring home one B and all the rest A's, they say I'm goofing off; if it's all A's, they think I'm studying too hard and should be more social, have more friends. I can't win!"

A girl chimes in, "My parents have made me take the SATs *four times*. Now they say if my scores don't go up a hundred points next time I'm not getting the car for the rest of the year."

I've had kids in class with their fingernails bitten to the

quick and looking miserable, feeling they have to get A's, and their parents going to the point of rewriting their papers for them. Every fall, T.C. is gripped by "Ivy League fever." Sweatshirts marked "Harvard" or "Princeton" start appearing. At the annual fall "college night," when representatives of 200 colleges and universities are available to meet prospective applicants, it's always the Ivy League reps who are swamped. In the fall of '84, the line of kids to see the man from Brown went halfway down the corridor. Of course, two-thirds of the kids in that line didn't have a prayer of entering an Ivy League school. They'd been pushed into applying by their parents. I got so fed up that one day in class I horrified everybody by saying I had yet to see anybody wearing an Ivy League sweatshirt get into an Ivy League school. The sweatshirts went back into drawers after that.

Kitty Porterfield, whose daughter Debbie went to Harvard after T.C., says she became the center of attention at local cocktail parties after the word got around. But it's not a status she appreciates. "It's like asking what kind of car you drive," says she. "It turns college into another piece of merchandise, and completely takes the kid out of it."

Associated with the middle-class obsession with achievement is something we call the "Not My Son Syndrome." Other children fail tests or skip classes, but not *my* son. It seems to afflict especially adults who are used to making the rules and getting their way. A high-ranking Pentagon official tore into young math teacher Marty Nickley after his son got a D. When Marty refused to change the grade, the officer tried to pull rank. He'd see that "something was done." The next day the kid apologized for his father's clumsy attempt at intimidation. "I deserved the grade and Dad knew it," he said.

Shortly before graduation one year, a member of the school board tried to push through a change in the requirement for honors diplomas. This totally disinterested representative of the school community proposed lowering the minimum grade point average required from 3.5 to 3.0. Everyone knew the board member's son had a GPA of 3.3. "It takes a board with a 2.0 mentality to make 3.0 an honors diploma," quipped guidance counselor Patricia Butts.

I feel sorry for such parents. They don't seem to realize that stepping in on the side of a kid who's in the wrong doesn't do the kid any favors. In their desire to make "better products" of their children, they're denying—or attempting to deny—their children's right to take responsibility for their own failures and, perhaps, raising doubts in kids' minds about whether they can make it on their own. It's as Bettelheim says later in his essay on families: a parent who is mainly interested in a child's achievement puts a weapon in that child's hands. That weapon is failure.

By the time kids reach high school, families are dealing with a youth culture that has its own powerful mores and values and is inaccessible to adults. Parents who are ambivalent, or hypocritical, about their convictions and beliefs at that point are in for trouble. Our guidance counselors all have first-hand evidence of the retreat—rout might be a better word—of parents.

A mother telephones. She wants a *guidance counselor* to tell her son that he can't take the car next weekend. An agitated parent rings up just before school starts. She wants a *counselor* to persuade a recalcitrant son who's sleeping off a hangover to catch the bus to school. A single, divorced mother comes to us for help with her fifteen-year-old daughter who's been "taking off whenever she likes and shacking up with a guy who's twenty-one." We find out later that the girl was just copying her mother's behavior. Mom has been disappearing with her boyfriend on weekends, leaving her two teen-age daughters to look after themselves.

Another mother wants to be her daughter's best friend. When the girl skips classes for weeks and announces plans to marry the latest in a long line of ne'er-do-well boyfriends, her mom takes it as a personal betrayal rather than a reflection on her parenting. "How could she do this to *me*," the mother sulks. "We were always so close, such good friends. I treated her like a sister. The two pregnancies and abortions were bad enough—but *this*!"

Nothing exposes parental confusion and weakness more vividly than the way a lot of families handle the drinking issue. Heavy drinking and partying have become widespread even among young teen-agers, in part because parents have caved in to the old con line that seldom fooled our mothers and fathers: "Everybody's doing it."

Principal Hanley remembers a father who wanted to serve alcohol at a party for the cast of the school play. When Hanley told him he'd be contributing to the delinquency of minors, the father protested that Hanley was "not in tune with what's going on." He said, "These kids have worked so hard. They deserve a rest."

The annual Stotesbury Crew Regatta in Philadelphia, at which T. C. Williams competes, is always one of the extracurricular highlights of the year. Some of the leading political and social lights of the Alexandria community go up to see their children row. But Hanley finally stopped attending. Parents were serving beer, wine, and hard liquor to kids and other parents at tailgate parties, and Hanley felt the presence of school officials would just seem to condone this kind of "entertainment." The attitude of many parents is summed up by the mother who excuses the drinking of even eighth-graders at parties in her home. "I'd rather have them do it at my house than somewhere else," she says.

More than drinking or drugs, sex is probably the element in the '80s youth culture that poses the biggest challenge to families and schools. Decisions about sex—when to become sexually active, how to take responsibility for birth control, and so on—require clear thinking about personal values. If there's any part of teen-agers' lives in which they need guidance, support, and information, this is obviously it. How teen-agers handle the emotional pressures of sex is bound to affect their academic performance and emotional well-being. Yet there's widespread evidence, in our community and beyond, that parental values on this subject just aren't being adequately transmitted.

"There's no communication about sex. No one says not to do it, and by default they're condoning it," twelfth-grader Marc Tillman told me. Kids tell me that most parents either don't want to know about the sexual activities of their youngsters or find the whole subject too painful to face. "My father jokes about sex with me," a seventeen-year-old girl confided. "He says if I get my driver's license, there'll probably be a lot of trouble with used rubbers in the ashtrays. He doesn't know I really *am* doing it. My mother won't talk about it at all even though I'm almost positive she knows."

Sexual curiosity and experimentation are a natural part of growing up, and even the strongest families have always found sex a difficult subject. What's made this a serious problem instead of just an awkward subject is the considerable evidence that children are becoming sexually active earlier than ever before, long before they're emotionally equipped to handle the tremendous emotional pressures that come with sex.

"Even eighth-grade girls have to know they can turn a guy on," Family Life instructor Joan Myers says. National surveys suggest that "only" a third of the girls and half of boys between the ages of fifteen and seventeen are sexually active.

But research data on sexual behavior is notoriously unreliable. Our school nurse, Marianne Heil, is one who believes the figures are too low. "We've raised these kids to be sexual characters," she says. "Sex is where it's at for them."

Heil is an irreverent, witty woman whose generous, open way with people encourages kids to talk freely about intimate, personal matters. Middle-class girls, she says, are "consciously sexually active," but seldom inform their parents. These girls, says Heil, are efficient and well organized in the way they handle their sex lives. They come to her for the phone numbers of Planned Parenthood, take their birth control pills faithfully and are well informed about the risks of pregnancy and VD. "If you don't have your rubber all you're going to get from a girl is oral sex," a twelfth-grade guy told me. When word got around that the mother of Janet Peyton, '85, worked for Planned Parenthood, girls began flocking to Janet to see if they could get confidential appointments with her mom. "It shocked me to see all the girls who were sexually active. The types I never would have suspected," said Janet.

"According to TV, you'd think *everybody* under sixteen had done it," says Chris Farris, who was president of the student council in 1984–85. "As much as there's pressure to drink, there's pressure to have sex."

Today's culture not only sends the message that it's okay to do it, it also provides a place to do it. That place is home. Jean Hunter, who teaches our Family Life course, always hears a ripple of laughter when she slips and talks about people losing their virginity in "the backseats of cars." Nowadays, that's more likely to happen at home during parents' work hours. "We're out of school at two and our parents don't come home till six," says Farris. "A lot of kids go home and call their moms to make sure they're still at work.

Then they go and do it."

It takes strong, active support from the family for a popular, attractive teen-ager to resist these pressures. Lani Thompson, a tall, statuesque brunette with a sort of punk hairstyle, has that. During her senior year, she socialized, dated, and attended parties with her friends. The difference was that Lani decided to keep her virginity. Her values on sex and other matters (she is also a non-drinker) came from her Mormon mother. "I tell my mother all," she said. She credits her mother with persuading her to take a stand on the issue of sex. When Lani was fifteen, she'd been dating the same guy for a year and he was demanding that they sleep together. Her mother confronted her about the relationship. She told Lani she was too young for intercourse.

"She said that if I was not going to listen to this advice, she would take me to a doctor for birth control. 'If you get pregnant, you're going to have the baby and I'll have to take care of it,' she told me. It made me realize how young I was. I dumped the guy."

Lani acknowledges that she sometimes feels "left out." But there are a lot of payoffs. She does not have curfews, as do a lot of other kids with less trusting parents. She feels she's gained the respect of her friends and classmates. And she's convinced that she's avoided a lot of the emotional stress that comes from a series of "heavy" relationships. "I get upset when I see friends losing their virginity to some guy they've just met," Lani says. "Losing your virginity has gotten to be like taking the SATs—you have to do it to get ready for college. But then they come to me after some guy's dumped them and say, 'I wish I hadn't done it.' "

When you consider some of the consequences of the apparent increase in sexual activity among young teen-agers in Alexandria, the traditional values of Lani's mother make a lot of sense. The most serious repercussion, of course, is an unplanned pregnancy. Marianne Heil began keeping careful track several years ago of the pregnancies of girls at T.C. and the two junior highs. In 1982–83, she counted fifty. In 1983–84, seventy-five. And near the end of the 1984–85 school year, the count had reached 115.

It so happens that all but a few of these girls come from low-income black families. By graduation in 1985, nearly one out of four black girls at T.C. had become pregnant since the previous September. White and black girls are engaging in sex earlier. But there is one difference. Poor black kids are much less likely to use birth control; and when a pregnancy results, they are far less apt to end it with an abortion.

Nobody is more concerned about the plight of single black teen-age mothers than national black organizations and leaders. Some of these, such as the Alpha Phi Alpha Fraternity, Inc., actively promote "parenting prevention" through the use of birth control by black teen-age boys. (Otha Myers, one of our black male counselors, is an active member of Alpha Phi Alpha.) These groups recognize better than anyone the social dynamite that illegitimate births are planting in cities all over America. In 1982, one out of four black babies was born to a teen-ager, nearly ninety percent of whom were unmarried. As the 1985 *State of Black America* report of the national Urban League noted: "The very characteristics that typify many teen-agers and that lead to so many pregnancies—impulsiveness, inability to plan effectively, lack of any clear goals in life—are the very opposite of those characteristics that are most needed in a parent." In other words, a new generation of poorly qualified parents is arriving on the scene, with all that means for schools and society in the next twenty years.

The reasons for the continuing high rate of out-of-wedlock

births to black teen-agers are enormously complex and subject to much debate—debate often burdened with political and racial preconceptions and prejudices. Black teen-agers have told me that their religious convictions cause them to reject abortion as a means of birth control. Many seem firmly in the right-to-life camp. I've seen girls coming to class in the eighth month of their pregnancy wearing big T-shirts declaring in large letters, "Choose Life."

Black organizations contend that rising unemployment among black men is the main factor that drives them to desert pregnant girlfriends. According to this view, the economic situation has undercut the ability of young black males to be family providers. Between 1960 and 1982, the percentage of employed black males dropped from seventy-four percent to fifty-two percent. With these rates of unemployment it is hardly surprising that black male teen-agers assume they cannot support the children they create.

Whatever the causes, black teen-age pregnancies pose enormous practical and philosophical problems for our school. On the practical side, the Alexandria schools are doing what they can to discourage very young girls from getting pregnant accidentally. The Family Life course, which I will describe in a moment, is a serious attempt to provide information and make students examine the consequences of pregnancy. At the same time, people like Marianne Heil use quiet persuasion when the chance arises. For example, she deduced from talks with some of the pregnant girls that they and their boyfriends were sometimes getting carried away at parties after basketball games. So, at the start of the 1984–85 season, Heil sat down with one member of the team and had a heart-to-heart talk about contraception. He promised to talk to the players about taking precautions. In mid-January, he reported to Heil that the team was "doing a good job" with the "prevent defense" she had mapped out. He wasn't referring to the team's performance on the court, and Heil was pleased with her coaching.

T.C. provides special support for girls who do get pregnant. The "School Age Parent" course, which meets two hours a week for twelve weeks, covers such topics as child nutrition, the birth process and post-natal care. It is intended to prepare teen-age mothers and prospective mothers for their roles. There has even been some discussion about setting up a day-care center at the school for the babies of students.

Yet, in our "progressive" response to teen pregnancy, we are caught between two fundamentally conflicting respon-sibilities—that of helping girls who need us and that of up-holding generally-accepted values. Regulations forbid excluding pregnant girls from school, and for some very good reasons. The vast majority of teen-age mothers who drop out never finish their education. Nobody wants to see these girls stigmatized or punished, as they once might have been. In helping pregnant girls, schools are assuming the role of fam-ily supporter that society plainly wants them to play.

But this still leaves some troubling questions. In remain-ing morally neutral while supporting increasing numbers of pregnant girls and ignoring the responsibility of the young fathers, are we copping out? Worse, are we sending the wrong message to other young people who are looking to us for moral guidance?

The school system tends to gloss over the central moral issue, which is not sexual promiscuity but accountability. Of the teen-age girls in the School Age Parent course, teacher Jeff Wilson says: "These are kids having kids. They're not into motherhood. Most go back to the normal teen-age life afterward—the partying and the dates with new guys."

"These young girls are pregnant and proud of it," says Jim McClure. "It dismays me to see them marching around like madonnas, wearing T-shirts with arrows pointing to 'Le Bébé.' " Jim McClure is a compassionate man who's devoted to kids. However, Jim says he is worried that the presence of these girls communicates the message to other kids that it's all right, when it plainly isn't—when the vast majority of these mothers have neither the maturity nor the financial stability to give a child what it needs.

Marianne Heil says her firsthand experiences as school nurse changed her attitude on this matter. "When I first began this job, I was a bleeding heart. I thought it was neat the way we accepted the pregnant girls and didn't point fingers. But the numbers just kept growing because no one said it was shameful to bring another human being into the world without caring for it. [We have] a sorority of pregnant girls. Baby showers. Classmates who are vying to be godparents. But once the baby's delivered, it's the end of the conversation. They never talk about it. When they're pregnant it's like being a star. Then they often shelve it with a mother or aunt. There's absolutely no reason *not* to get pregnant. Why take pills? They make you gain weight. They bloat you. And an IUD 'hurts.' They get their ADC [welfare] check, free health care and food stamps, no financial worries."

Of the fathers, Jeff Wilson says: "They hang around for a while, visit the kid, but soon drop out. There's seldom any long-term involvement, and very few marriages." Several times I've heard seventeen-year-old fathers in my English class boast that they were good parents because they visit their children once a week and give the mother "Pampers" money.

For a lot of poor young black males, it seems that the possible consequences of sex are not important. The tradition of fatherhood seems absent. Many of them have had no real fathers themselves. It's kind of a joke with them. When my wife was pregnant with our first baby, a couple of guys I taught quipped that their then thirty-nine-year-old English teacher was "way behind." "I've already got two," said one seventeen-year-old boy. And the Baby Doctor was a hero to a lot of boys in his class. Black girls I've known from English class tell me most boys deny parenthood. "Get out of my face, bitch! That ain't my kid," one girl quoted her boyfriend as saying when she confronted him with his paternity.

If it is not the school's place to pass moral judgment, it is its *duty* to stand for values. That is why some teachers and school officials have begun to have second thoughts about programs that support an increasing number of pregnant girls while appearing to remain neutral about conduct that has such devastating consequences for all of society.

Alexandria's pioneering Family Life program is the school system's response to this crisis. Beginning in 1983–84, Family Life became a required full-year program for all ninth-graders (except those whose families express "moral or religious" objections). Ninth-graders who miss the course because of some legitimate academic conflict must take it when they get to T.C. the next year. Family Life has overwhelming support from the community, thanks to several years of preparation with parents, teachers, the school board, and public health agencies, in a way that reassured families that Family Life would not be "imposing" values on anybody.

At one level, Family Life is sex education. It provides all the usual biological and health information and attempts to clear up common misperceptions (such as "You can't get pregnant the first time"). During the year, it takes up such subjects as rape, abortion, homosexuality, masturbation, teen-age pregnancy, and sex in ads.

Not only are the girls and boys taught that it's okay to say "no," but they're also taught *how* to say it. Teachers set up real-life situations and play out roles. Family Life instructor

Jean Hunter sometimes plays the part of the girl and a student plays her boyfriend.

HUNTER: We're alone, we've been in a clinch, and I push you back. I say, 'No, I don't want to.'
STUDENT: But the time is now.
HUNTER: Not for me.
STUDENT: It's got to be.
HUNTER: That's a decision I have to make for myself.
STUDENT: But I'm right for you.
HUNTER: I care about you but I'm not ready to have sex yet.
STUDENT: I can help you make the decision now.
HUNTER: It's not your decision to make.
STUDENT: It can be.
HUNTER: You're playing like you have magical powers.

Afterward Hunter explains, "It's not enough to tell girls it's all right to say no. We have to actually give them the words to say it with." Out of this kind of discussion can come an awareness that sex involves choices and individual responsibility—that it's not something that just happens.

It's too early to say whether such courses dramatically reduce teen-age pregnancies. Halfway through the 1984–85 year, a ninth-grader in Joan Myers's class announced sheepishly that she was pregnant. She didn't want to use birth control, she said, because it might have seemed that she had planned in advance to have sex with her boyfriend instead of its just happening. By her perverse logic, she'd gotten pregnant in order to preserve her reputation. It was a setback for Joan.

Family Life is more than sex ed. It's a course that helps parents and kids communicate about ethics and values, birth, life, death, and dying. One of the most interesting parts of the program involves sending the kids home with an assignment to interview their parents about *their* childhood. Family Life has helped a lot of families open up with each other. It's proved beyond a shadow of a doubt that the most profound and personal topics have a place in public schools.

Some might ask, nevertheless, why it is the place of a public school to devote time that could be spent on academics to such courses. There was a time when I asked that question myself. I'm old-fashioned enough to have snickered and joined in the jokes in the faculty lounge about sex ed. I still wonder if the course really should last an entire year. Couldn't the material be covered in a semester? And is it necessary to expose ninth- and tenth-graders to the vogueish "psychobabble" that sometimes slips into the discussions? Some Family Life teachers remind me of the nuns who drilled me on the catechism in grammar school!

But these are the reservations of a "traditional" teacher in his forties. As I've observed the impact of divorce and the youth culture on kids, I've come to realize that courses such as Family Life are a necessary response by the schools to a tremendous need in families and children. Kids desperately want to discuss personal values. Schools, increasingly, are the only forum for such exploration. I think the advocates of sex ed, and the advocates of prayer in the school, have much more in common than they acknowledge. Both are saying that schools have a role to play in the development of a child's character and deepest values. The issue isn't really whether or not to pray in schools. It's whether schools can afford not to provide an education in matters about which society and all religions are in basic agreement: personal responsibility, honesty, self-discipline, and other qualities of character.

I believe that most of the families we serve *want* schools to do more than process their children for college or jobs like a factory. They want and expect them to provide an education in values. They want them to care about their children's emotional as well as intellectual development. Even the obsession that so many parents have with grades and achievement hides, I think, their *real* concern: "Is my child okay— does he or she have the personal qualities, the character and the emotional stuff that I know from my own experience are necessary to lead a successful life?"

Yet we cannot accept the whole responsibility. The trade-off for schools doing more to help support the harried families of the '80s has to be a much greater willingness on the part of families to do their share. We can't take over, as some seem to expect.

There have been several remarkable examples in Alexandria of what parents and teachers can accomplish together. Parents of kids in the junior high schools had known for some time that the partying of thirteen- and fourteen-year-olds was reaching epic proportions. But many parents felt isolated and powerless to do anything. In the fall of 1984, Joyce and Dick Gordon agreed to let their thirteen-year-old daughter Pam give a party at their home. The Gordons are good parents, and Pam is a responsible young person. Before the party, Pam warned her mother to lock up the liquor. Joyce and Dick conscientiously greeted all the guests—making sure they were carrying no liquor—then escorted them to the basement party room and mingled there as chaperones. As the basement entertainment went on, Joyce was puzzled to note that the kids were leaving and entering the house frequently. Finally a neighbor called saying young people were drinking outside. When Dick checked, he found the street strewn with broken wine bottles and beer cans which had been secreted away in the surrounding bushes before the party started. At that point, Joyce and her husband called the party guests together, threatened to call the police if the drinking continued, and ordered those who had drunk too much to call their parents. A soused thirteen-year-old collapsed at their feet. A lot of the parents of the young drunks were never the wiser. The inebriated kids shrewdly called C.A.R.S. (Catch A Ride Safely, a student-run taxi service to help the inebriated) for a lift instead of phoning home.

When Joyce called the school to report what had happened, she found out that a group of *teachers* was already working to bring the partying under control. In addition to sporadic reports from parents, teachers had received complaints from kids who felt pressured into drinking by leaders of the party clique. For several weeks, history teacher Jack Esformes, English teacher Nancy Howard and half a dozen others telephoned ninety families to alert them to the drinking and ask for ideas. Meetings of parents, teachers and some kids in homes and schools ensued. The generation gap quickly became apparent when parental suggestions for pumpkin-carving parties and tug-of-war contests were hooted down by sophisticated adolescents. But the parents did not back away from their determination to stick together. They signed pledges that no liquor would be served at parties, which, they agreed, would be carefully chaperoned.

The effort was not an unqualified success. Afterward, teachers and parents acknowledged, some adolescents continued to drink, and others boycotted the planned events, which included a hayride and a church dance sponsored by the adults. Yet the experience showed parents and teachers that they were not powerless. Parents reinforced each others' values and no longer felt alone against a hundred kids. And it helped relieve some of the social pressure on the kids.

Teacher Nancy Howard said later that she had been worried at first that parents would think she was meddling in family matters. Instead, she said, the families were extremely grateful. "All of us were so impressed by the caring attitude of these teachers, with the fact that they took the lives of our children beyond the classroom very seriously," said Carol LaSasso, whose thirteen-year-old daughter was among the first to bring the drinking to the attention of teachers.

A favorite poem of my students is always Richard Wilbur's "The Writer," a rumination about his young daughter's growing up. He recalls a "dazed starling" trapped in his daughter's room. As he and his daughter stood at the entrance of the room, they were aware that the bird would have to find its *own* way out through the open window.

> . . . for a helpless hour, through the crack of the door,
> We watched the sleek, wild, dark
>
> And iridescent creature
> Batter against the brilliance, drop like a glove
> To the hard floor, or the desk-top,
>
> And wait then, humped and bloody,
> For the wits to try it again . . .

Finally the bird lifted off from a chair and made it through the window, "clearing the sill of the world."

Of course, the poem is about parenting and the helplessness parents often feel as they realize there is only so much they can do for their children. It touches a deep truth seemingly forgotten by many anxious middle-class parents. Pressure and incessant demands on kids won't enable them to soar away from their adolescence into an independent adulthood. Great parents give their children encouragement, support, and detailed attention, but they also find ways to let them know they have to grow up on their own.

Some families manage to do this even in the trying conditions of the '80s. The Porterfields are a local family that is doing just that. Jovan Porterfield grew up in the late Depression in Waxahachie, Texas—scene of the 1984 Sally Field movie *Places in the Heart*. He attended North Texas State College—one of the first in his family to make it beyond high school. Later, he and his wife Kitty managed to pass on his own strongest lesson from his hard-times Texas childhood: Everybody has to pull together.

The Porterfields seem engagingly indifferent to the usual trappings of middle-class success. Kitty jokes about the porch that's falling down and the lawn that indulgent neighbors sometimes feel compelled to mow after it's been neglected for weeks. Jovan quit a high-paying job with an electronics corporation because he didn't like attending black-tie banquets where salesmen had to play the corporate game. He has done well enough in Alexandria real estate, and Kitty, who graduated from Radcliffe in 1963, has been a coordinator for the Arlington Humanities Project. She's been active in the life of T. C. Williams, working on committees, and is around the school a lot. But neither is among the community's movers and shakers.

They've been fortunate with their kids. Karen, class of '81, is the creative one—the seeker. As I write this, she's studying theology at a university in India, after a year studying art history in London. Debbie, class of '83, is the brain. Several teachers rank her as one of the top two or three students who ever went through the school. She's halfway through Harvard now, following in her mother's footsteps, and majoring in biology. Michael, class of '85, is the leader. He was president of his class, co-captain of the varsity crew, and an all-state center on the football team.

When the children were young, Kitty and her husband would tell them, "You have to make it work when we're gone." Michael remembers that "they trusted us and we were kind of afraid to screw up." Debbie thinks she knows her mother's secret of success as a parent. "She never pushed me too much. When I had a decision to make she'd find the right people for me to talk to, but after that she'd drop out of the picture, even though I know it wasn't always easy."

The Porterfields are fun to be around, and can seem almost laid-back. Debbie says of her father, "He has this crazy sense of fun, of play, to him. Just by watching him we all learned that life is meant to be enjoyed, that you can't take things too seriously." But underneath there's an old-fashioned American toughness and independence—a willingness to stand up for principle. It comes through in Jovan's decision to quit his job, in both parents' support of Debbie when she began dating a black classmate and in other ways. I'm convinced the kids have picked up on it.

But it isn't the academic, athletic or creative achievements of these three that have impressed me as much as their human qualities—their warmth, character, integrity and love of life. Michael, a boy with an unusually smart older sister, could have turned into a resentful, withdrawn underachiever. Instead, he took delight in his sister's academic success and found ways to express his own personal strengths. Michael's dad encouraged him to go his own way. While most white middle-class fathers in Alexandria were pushing their sons into soccer, Jovan went along enthusiastically when Michael played football. In 1984, he was one of two whites on the starting team. A few years ago, Debbie began dating Steve Stanford, an extremely gifted black classmate now at Stanford University. When *The Washington Post* ran a picture of the two in the library in connection with an article on high school romances, the Porterfields got hate calls. But the Porterfields stood by Debbie and Steve. "Just be yourself," Kitty told her daughter.

.   .   .

Whenever I get a parental anxiety attack, wondering whether I'm doing enough with and for *my* children at home, it helps to think about the success of other parents who have had to face much bigger obstacles than I. It puts things in perspective for me to think about the Wellingtons, who've sent numerous children through T.C.

Sixteen years ago, Hattie Mae and Luther Wellington from Wilson, North Carolina, gathered their eleven children into a borrowed station wagon and headed for Alexandria, where Luther had found a construction job. Hattie Mae moved reluctantly. She feared that city life might corrupt her children. Sharon, the youngest, says the people of Wilson "thought we'd end up sweeping streets or in jail."

In Alexandria, the Wellingtons were ostracized at first by their black neighbors as a tribe of country people. "Every afternoon a crowd of children was waiting outside of Robert E. Lee School to beat us up," recalls Angela, the second-youngest. "They didn't like us because we were so different, with our country accents, and in the beginning, we didn't have the nicest clothes."

Sixteen years after those inauspicious beginnings, the Wellington family has not only survived but flourished. Six of the children have or soon will have their college degrees; seven are ministers. When you ask any of the Wellington children how they beat the odds, you always get the same answer: "Our mother and the church."

"When we first came to Alexandria the church was our refuge," says Angela, a 1982 University of Virginia graduate. "Our family were really outcasts—there were so many of us and we were so poor—and the church was the only place where we really felt accepted."

"My mother saw to it that we were either in school, in church, or in the house," says Sharon, who entered Georgetown University in the fall of 1984. "She never gave us any time to get into any real trouble. She never set goals for me but had this clever way of somehow making me set them for myself. I think the thing that sticks out the most about my mother is the fact that she was always there for us. No matter how tired she was—and she worked long hours as a maid cleaning white ladies' houses—she always made time for us. When my turn came she was there."

Now it's Hattie Mae Wellington's turn. In 1981, she took a graduate equivalency test and became the twelfth member of her family to get a high school diploma. In June 1984, she got an associate degree at Northern Virginia Community College, and she plans to transfer to a four-year college to seek a degree in counseling. She should finish college just one year before Sharon graduates from Georgetown.

Hattie Mae Wellington never had any trouble communicating her values to her children.

4

Together but Unequal

Whenever I teach a class of Phase 1 twelfth-graders—those with reading skills of sixth-graders or below—I always show *The Miracle Worker*, the movie in which Patty Duke plays the part of the blind and deaf Helen Keller. I've probably seen it fifty times by now, but I'm still moved when Anne Sullivan, the teacher, breaks through and shows Helen how to communicate. Maybe if Anne Sullivan found a way to get through, American schools can find a way to reach the thousands of poor black kids who don't read well.

Of all the statistics we gather about students at T. C. Williams, the most discouraging are those that measure the ability to read. Nearly half the 960 tenth-graders who came to us from Alexandria's two junior high schools in the fall of 1985 were reading below grade level. More than a hundred read no better than sixth-graders, and a few were at the level of children in first or second grade: they could understand street signs and some newspaper headlines, but not a newspaper story about, say, last Sunday's Redskins game. They have trouble pronouncing or understanding words such as "silence," "courage," "distant," and "region."

As a group, T.C.'s black students do not rank well on national tests. When examined in 1985, our black eleventh-graders averaged in the bottom twenty percent on the Science Research Associates test of reading skills. T.C.'s whites averaged in the top thirty percent. Only three of the twenty-three black seniors on our 1984 state championship football team would have been eligible to play as college freshmen if

the proposed National Collegiate Athletic Association requirement of a combined SAT math and verbal score of 700
had been in effect.

This bleak situation is not unique to Alexandria. Nationwide, three out of five blacks who took the Scholastic Aptitude Test in the 1983–84 school year scored below 350 on
the verbal part of the exam, which measures vocabulary and
reading; for whites it was only one out of three. From my
experience, students with scores in the 350 range can't handle rigorous high school work, let alone rigorous college
courses. And these figures are only for the thirteen percent
of all black eighteen-year-olds nationwide who took the
test—a group that comprises most of the college-bound and
relatively advanced students.

As a teacher, I see the tragedies behind these numbers. I'll
never forget the witty, gregarious star athlete who was popular with teachers and students alike. One day he came to
me with a request: Could I read him a newspaper account of
his exploits in a recent sports contest? There was the Phase
1 reader who had teachers worried that he wouldn't be able
to understand airport signs on his way to visit colleges that
were recruiting him with offers of an athletic scholarship.

A casual visitor to our school might easily conclude that
we are practicing deliberate racial segregation. He'd see
mostly whites in the physics lab and mostly blacks in the
Career Wing. He'd see Phase 1 English classes made up almost entirely of blacks, and advanced English classes with
only a few black faces in them. Of the eighty-nine students
who took my advanced placement English course for college
credit in 1983–84, only seven were black, and five of them
tried to drop out—this in a school in which black and white
enrollments are almost equal.

Yet there's no master plan I know of to keep the races and
classes apart; it just works out that way. "Phasing," "special

education," "vocational education," "gifted and talented programs" in the earlier grades, and the college-level advanced placement courses all have the effect, intended or not, of keeping poor minority kids with academic problems separate from middle-class kids who are seeking a traditional high school education before college.

I confess to tremendous feelings of ambivalence about teaching seventeen-year-olds who read like ten-year-olds. On the one hand, these pupils don't seem like hopeless cases from a lost underclass. They don't fit the common stereotype of the slow-talking, malnourished, "dull" student. The poverty programs have helped smooth over the rough edges of their poverty. Food stamps, the welfare safety net and school lunch programs have put food in their stomachs and clothes on their backs. There is a new class of poor and disadvantaged in the electronic age. They seem well nourished and even able to afford some of life's "luxuries," from dope to ghetto blasters. Except when they lapse into street dialect, saying "be" for "are," "mines" for "mine" and of course the ubiquitous adjective "motherf——," our deficient readers are all but indistinguishable from other students. They're talkative, street wise, socially at ease, funny, and sensitive. They're certainly not "dumb" or "dull" in any conventional sense. They can argue a teacher down on the fine points. A lot of these kids are more interesting, open, and honest than the "grinds" in my advanced English classes. They usually leave a lasting impression on me. When I run into former "tormenters" such as Willie, Carl, and Gene at a supermarket or a ball game years after they've left my classroom, there's an instant rapport. We're glad to see each other, and we often laugh about the bad old days.

Nonetheless, these kids are deprived. Sophisticated as many of them seem, something's missing. Our white middle class kids are bored with school, but they play the game, get their B's and A's, because they know there's something in it for them—a college acceptance, a job, or the use of the family car for the weekend. These incentives don't seem to operate in the culture of the majority of our poor readers. The Jesse Jackson message—to pull oneself up by the bootstraps, that hard work has its rewards—apparently doesn't get through. When you ask them what their expectations for the future are, they'll tell you they plan to bag groceries or work for fast food restaurants. I'm no reading expert, but you hardly have to be one to question whether these ambitions stimulate the motivation needed to succeed in school. How often have I heard, "I don't need this—I've already got a job," or "It ain't gonna do me no good!"

It's this attitude that makes teaching these kids so frustrating. There's an unwritten rule in our English Department: no teacher will be assigned more than two periods a day of Phase 1 students. Several years ago, before this was the case, I had three such classes one year. Night after night I'd drive home feeling angry and guilty. Was it a cop-out to give them passing grades? Was it racist to let them slide through, on grounds that a lone teacher couldn't make a difference? Why didn't the school system do something about these kids? Before the year was out, I seriously considered quitting the teaching profession.

I got through the year, but I didn't get over my frustrations. Our curriculum guide describes Phase 1 instruction as being "designed for students with reading scores of 1.0 (starting first grade) to 6.9 (ending sixth grade)." The guide says that work will be "organized" to help the students achieve skills such as forming complete sentences and using a dictionary. But how can we teach the use of dictionaries to students who can't recognize many words longer than two syllables? Despite the high-flown description of the "organized" Phase 1 instruction, in practice Phase 1 teachers fall back on whatever keeps the students busy and quiet, whether it's grammar exercises they forget in a week, or the film *Dracula*.

Avoiding Phase 1 classes is one of the games that English teachers play at T.C. Some of the twenty-five teachers in the English department get out of teaching them by saying they simply can't handle them—and, indeed, many don't have the temperament. Others suffer in varying degrees of silence. "I'm going to work at Bloomingdale's if I have to teach these kids again" is a remark I've heard in the faculty lounge. Yet teachers seldom complain about the foreign students who are substandard readers. "Why can't the black kids be like *them*," is a comment that virtually all of us have let slip.

We hear a lot about the "tracking" of students into fast and slow classes. We hear less about another phenomenon: the tracking of *teachers*. In principle, the kids with the most problems should be getting the best teachers. In practice, the system operates just the opposite way. While good teachers are usually rewarded with good students, the incompetent or rebellious are punished with the worst. "Given the fact that it's almost impossible to fire horrible teachers, you assign them to the kids whose parents will complain the least. That ends up being the lower class," an administrator once acknowledged to me.

The truth is that even the best teachers have given up on these black kids. For years, I have fought against this attitude in myself. But I felt I was losing the battle in the Phase 1 English class of twelfth-graders I had in 1982–83. By Thanksgiving, I was teaching over an incessant background murmur. A group of black kids on one side of the class baited several foreign students. "He smells." "He's a faggot." I had to jump between them to prevent a fight and I was constantly worried that I'd really lose my temper—the way I did a few years ago when a girl started a fight and I punted her purse down the hall, an emotional outburst that earned me a well-deserved reprimand from the school administration. Several were on drugs; one boy veered between depression and hyperactivity, sitting silently one day and pinching girls the next; another boy who had just gotten his girlfriend pregnant and was attending a class for prospective fathers, on several occasions threatened to "get me" when I asked him to stop talking to the girls around him. By the spring semester, some of the students simply refused to do the assignments work because they were convinced that they could stop working and still get a D for the year.

The next year, the head of the English department saw to it that my two Phase 1 classes were smaller, and she told me I would probably find teaching eleventh-graders easier. They *were* easier to work with, but I still felt frustrated. In a regular class of eleventh-graders, I normally have students read books such as *The Catcher in the Rye*, *Native Son*, and *Huckleberry Finn*. But these books were far beyond the ability of my Phase 1 kids. The problem wasn't that they couldn't "relate" to the characters of J. D. Salinger, Richard Wright and Mark Twain. I tried them on a book that should have been very relevant to the black students who made up a majority of the class: *I Know Why the Caged Bird Sings*, the autobiography of black dancer and writer Maya Angelou. After a few days, I began hearing the old refrain: "It's boring"—which, as I have said, is usually a code phrase for "I can't read it." I tried *Superstars of Soul*, a book with sixteen short biographies of singers, followed by vocabulary and reading comprehension exercises. They went wild over the chapter on Michael Jackson. They liked the one on Teddy Prendergast. But soon I began hearing it again: "It's boring."

In the fall of 1984, the English department must have sensed my exasperation, for I was "promoted" to two classes of Phase 2 twelfth-graders, who are "only" two to five grades behind in their reading ability. The teacher who got my two

Phase 1 classes was furious, and tried to get his Phase 2 classes back, but the administration stuck to its decision.

Compared to those in the unruly Phase 1 classes, these kids were quiet and attentive. A number of them tried to do their work; they had larger vocabularies and could follow a story much better. At first I was excited about the possibilities of working with these pupils, because I sensed they were tantalizingly close to being adequate students. But the longer I taught them, the more I was aware of the subtle difficulties. Most of them had trouble understanding irony or satire, and couldn't read between the lines to recognize motives and feelings implied by dialogue. In the *Catcher in the Rye* scene in which Holden Caulfield visits a prostitute and introduces himself with the pseudonym Jim Steele, the Phase 2 students wanted to know "what happened to Caulfield."

This teaching required constant repetition, review, and explanation of what was going on in the story or poem we were studying. I started them on *Song of Solomon*, which dealt with a young black man's struggle to make sense of his family history. They were interested, but most of them still had great difficulty comprehending it. After several weeks, some of them still could not sort out the family relationships. Meanwhile, several of the foreign students sailed ahead, getting A's on the tests and complaining I was going too slow.

While we were reading *Song of Solomon*, black students would frequently ask me, "I thought this was an *English* class—when do we start doing *English*?"

I got angry and said, "What do you think reading a novel is?"

They'd invariably reply, "When do we study *grammar*?"

I realized they had come to believe that English was the study of simple rules of grammar to be memorized and forgotten. Their teachers had resorted to that kind of rote, organized activity to keep them "busy." "All you can do is keep them quiet and hope they don't ruin your day," one teacher confided. Yet many of these students wanted to learn and had the ability to do so.

George Webber, a retired black teacher who taught at Alexandria's Parker-Gray High School in the '60s when it was a segregated black school, and later at T. C. Williams, anguishes over the academic deficiencies he sees in these students. "Black kids at T. C. Williams are in terrible shape. It brings tears to my eyes when I think how little they care about education. They seem scared to be in classes with whites, afraid they'll look dumb. A lot of them are all confused about achievement. They feel that if they study they'll become white."

It's bad enough that a great many students arrive at T. C. Williams not reading confidently. What's worse is that most of them graduate three years later without having overcome this deficiency. They'll walk down the aisle to receive their diploma on graduation day, the same as classmates bound for the University of Virginia and Dartmouth. But the appearance of equality will be misleading.

In 1954, the Supreme Court struck down segregated public education in America. It rejected the hypocrisy inherent in "separate but equal." Today, I fear, we have a system in which the education of blacks and whites could be described as "together but unequal."

Certainly these black students do not begin their education the academic equals of whites. In the spring of 1985, Alexandria's first graders took the Science Research Associates test in reading. Whites averaged in the seventy-fourth percentile nationally, while blacks averaged in the thirty-fifth. As black kids move through the school system, their progress on this test is amazingly predictable—so predictable, in fact, that school officials speak of the "Alexandria curve." For the first three grades, blacks slightly improve their ranking relative to others; but then they steadily lose ground until, by eleventh grade, they rank below where they started in first grade. Slightly more than half the blacks in the class of '85 had a D average, or worse.

Who's to blame? People teaching senior high school blame the junior highs, the junior highs blame the elementary schools, and everybody blames the families.

Deprived family backgrounds, peer pressures, and cultural and economic factors certainly do contribute to this situation. There is a remarkable correlation between test scores and family income. The average income of a black family in Alexandria is $14,700 a year, the lowest in the entire Washington area. In neighboring jurisdictions, where income of black families is somewhat higher, so are the test scores of black children.

Cultural factors are important, perhaps decisive. As Webber suggests, there's a strong "anti-achievement ethic" among poor black kids. "They identify achievement with whites and want no part of it," I was once told by William Carr, a black psychologist who gained his insights working as a counselor of young prisoners at the reformatory in Lorton, Virginia. "There were many young men in prison who had brilliant minds but read at a second grade level. Once they could face their problem without shame and see that learning was a real value, their progress was amazing."

Charlotte Stokes, head of the T. C. Williams social studies department, has special insights into the obstacles that "the street" places in the way of young blacks who want more from life than the street culture. She remembers the trouble it caused when she publicly praised a young black student for doing excellent work in her "special materials" class (the social studies equivalent of Phase 1 English). "He was furious that I recognized his achievement in front of his friends and came up after class and told me never to do it again. He tried to get even with me by coming late to class for the next week." Stokes thinks a lot of the bad behavior of poor blacks in class is "part of a highly stylized game of dumbness."

It would be unfair to suggest that schools have done nothing to improve the academic achievement of black children. There are, for starters, a number of federal and state programs, relics of President Lyndon Johnson's War on Poverty. The federal government spends about $2.2 million a year on the education of Alexandria kids, providing vocational training and various kinds of specialized aid for the handicapped and economically disadvantaged. The federal money pays for seventeen teachers, two teacher's aides and educational materials.

There's Head Start, which is for economically disadvantaged preschoolers. Seventy-five Alexandria children between three and five attend a Head Start program housed in one of the elementary schools. Head Start teachers with special training also visit twenty-five homes where children are living with their non-working mothers who are usually on welfare. The goal is to provide these youngsters with some of the intellectual stimulation and enrichment that middle-class children routinely get at home.

In addition, several important federal programs are available under Title I/Chapter 1 of the Elementary and Secondary Education Act, the legislation that for the first time brought the federal government into U.S. public schools in a big way. Children whom tests show to be behind in reading are eligible for the "educationally disadvantaged" program, in which some 900 Alexandria children in grades two through nine are enrolled. Usually a student spends one hour a day in a small group with a specially trained remedial reading teacher.

There's also "special education," set up under federal and state laws requiring schools to meet the needs of handicapped students with physical and emotional impairments. This includes the highly acclaimed "Learning Disabled" (LD) program, which provides in-school tutoring tailored to the needs of individual students. It offers many services, from assigning students to special schools to providing one-on-one tutoring.

Alexandria supplements those federal and state programs with some of its own. In seventh, eighth, and ninth grades, students who are two or more grade levels behind in their reading get special help from reading specialists. Part of the help consists of "follow up" visits to the students' classrooms to monitor their progress. There's also our new "holdover" system which, in theory, requires junior high school students to repeat courses they fail. Before students enter T. C. Williams, they take the Stanford Diagnostic Test. On the basis of that test, and the recommendations of their teachers, our guidance department groups the new students by ability. Those reading no better than sixth graders are placed in "basic math," "special materials" social sciences, and Phase 1 English.

On the surface, this looks impressive. There's just one problem: it doesn't make competent readers and communicators out of poor, disadvantaged black kids. Lots of money is spent; teachers are employed; and the school system displays the programs as proof that it's "trying to do something." But what counts are results, and for this generation of kids, evidence of really significant results isn't there. Perhaps there's no other way to achieve higher literacy goals; perhaps, as educators often say privately, "it will take a few more generations." Yet a closer look at some of the programs suggests we're not doing all we say we are.

Take Head Start. It's a good program, but it reaches only a

hundred kids a year in a city where hundreds more need the enrichment and stimulation it provides. Poverty experts estimate that, nationwide, Head Start reaches only one-third of the kids who need it. The problem, says Alexandria's Head Start coordinator, is that many truly disadvantaged children who should be in the program can't qualify because their parents earn too much money. Meanwhile hundreds of white preschool children attend church- or community-run private day care and "early education" centers.

Then there's the Learning Disabled program, which seems to get good results with kids who are not reaching their potential. Blacks far outnumber whites in the program (which is one of the few that goes to the end of high school), but getting into it is anything but automatic for the poor minority kids who desperately need help. The law states that the program is for the *handicapped*: those with perceptual handicaps, dyslexia, minimal brain dysfunction, or other "psychoneurological disabilities." According to the handbook for parents issued by the Alexandria schools, LD specifically is *not* for "children who have learning disabilities which are primarily the result of . . . environmental, cultural or economic disadvantage." Since the federal "educationally disadvantaged" reading program ends in ninth grade, there is no program for the economically disadvantaged *per se* at T.C. About 125 black students out of 1,100 (less than one in eight) are enrolled in LD. Yet close to three out of four blacks are reading below grade level. LD specialists say their hands are tied. Under the rules of the program, most of those students can't be admitted because they are performing as would be expected according to their IQ scores and therefore cannot be classified as having a "learning disability." LD teachers tell me that they could help these kids if there were some way to get them into LD classes.

The "holdover" program is also not quite as it seems. At

first blush, it seems to suggest that the schools are raising their expectations for minority students. When the school system announced in June 1984 that 150 seventh-graders (among whom were 115 blacks) were being made to repeat, there was a lot of media coverage. But the "held over" seventh-graders actually went on to eighth-grade courses, except for the one they had failed. Nothing changed but the labeling. Often they repeat the class they failed with the same teacher, the same materials, and no special help.

Jean Hunter, a highly regarded Alexandria teacher who taught poor readers for years in the Alexandria junior high schools, is discouraged by the results. "The reading programs in junior and senior high don't work. We were pressured to do something, so we did," she says. But the money was put in "at the wrong end." In her view the only hope is to reach kids early—well before they get to school. Hunter recently quit teaching reading and began teaching sex education because she felt she could make more of a contribution to solving the reading problem by persuading prospective teen-age mothers and young girls with children to provide mental stimulation for their infants at home.

Despite all the monitoring, testing, and extra help, a lot of students arrive at T.C. with little confidence in their ability to read or do basic math, and not much more when they leave. The education system's matching low expectations can be seen in a single fact: in the four years since Virginia seniors were required to pass a "minimum competency" test, only one T. C. Williams student was denied a diploma—even though many failed the test the first time around and some had to take it as often as five times. Yet hundreds have left our school reading below grade level.

The operating assumption is that students arriving at T. C. *can* read and it's too late to do much about it if they can't. In high school, the "help" programs thin out considerably. Until the fall of 1984, substandard readers at T. C. Williams spent an hour a *week* in the school's "reading lab," a relic of an earlier era's fascination with technical solutions to complex problems. That program, which was too superficial to have any lasting effect, was shut down in 1984.

Could we do better for students who are with us six hours a day, five days a week, forty weeks a year for three years of their lives? The obstacles are twofold. First, most teachers and administrators doubt that much can be done to improve reading ability after a teen-ager reaches tenth grade. Second, the school system never made an all-out commitment to the cause of black literacy for reasons that are rooted in politics and recent history. Since desegregation, the priority mission of the white-dominated school system has been to maintain the support of the middle class while complying with laws that require children of disparate backgrounds and abilities to attend schools together. Presented with the conflicting priorities of retaining white middle-class loyalties while desegregating the schools, schools evolved a system of sorting in which the bright were separated from the average and the average from the slow early in their education.

At the end of third grade, for example, students are selected for the Academically Talented Program on the basis of tests, psychological evaluations, teacher recommendations, and "parent nominations," in which parents complete a checklist of their eight-year-old's superior ability to "use keen observational skills," "use advanced vocabulary," and "set high standards for self." To say that this is a program tailored to the white middle class is a gross understatement. At Lyles-Crouch Elementary School, which has a black student majority, there were only five black children out of sixty-one in the ATP program in 1984. Throughout the Alexandria elementary schools, whites outnumber blacks in the program six to one.

Certainly the community needs programs that stimulate and challenge gifted students, and I don't doubt that Alexandria is blessed with more than its fair share of bright young people with "keen observational skills." But factors other than academic talent affect the selection of children for the program. Of the fifty-eight graduating seniors in T. C. Williams' class of '84 who were in the ATP program in elementary school, I'd say a dozen at most could be called truly "gifted." The others I'd call reasonably bright, nice kids. Some I'd classify as downright mediocre.

ATP is a middle-class program manipulated by middle-class families for their benefit, with the collusion of the school system. For years, one of the most powerful of the School Board's advisory groups has been its Gifted and Talented Committee, consisting of middle-class parents who, according to school officials, try to squeeze everything they can out of the system for their own children. ATP is filled with the sons and daughters of the political and social elite, some of whom are anything but elite when it comes to the academic ability of their kids. It's no secret that school counseling departments, which assign children to classes, group children by their socioeconomic background as well as by academic ability.

By the time kids reach high school, they've been pretty clearly separated into those who are presumed to be academic achievers and those for whom high school is expected to be a holding area until graduation. "Nobody wants to say it, but everyone knows that these kids are just marking time here, hanging around until they get their meaningless diploma," guidance counselor Otha Myers acknowledges.

One of the school's methods for dealing with this problem is to channel a lot of poor readers into a program that includes one to three hours a day of vocational courses: auto mechanics, electronics, carpentry, climate control (installing heating and air-conditioning systems), and cooking. The center of "voc ed" is the palatial $5 million "career wing." While the school is running out of classroom space, you could put fifteen classrooms in just the area of the career wing allocated to auto mechanics and printing. The auto section looks like the repair shop of a medium-sized car dealership. The equipment is so top-of-the-line that some teachers take their cars there to be repaired.

The career wing was built for a lofty motive: helping students develop skills that would get them jobs. But there is still much controversy about the wisdom of the voc ed program. Some of the skills being taught appear to be bordering on obsolescence. We are still teaching "printing" in a time when computers are rapidly taking over the jobs printers used to perform. The printing shop's most sophisticated machine is an offset press which, says teacher Tom McClay, can only be mastered by his best students. With automation and computerization of printing, the vast majority of his graduates will end up as "gophers doing the most basic jobs, like loading paper and ink. . . . Very few people know how bad off these kids are," says McClay. A personnel man from a local print shop told McClay after visiting one of his classes, "What you have here are the employable handicapped."

Labor unions and employers these days are looking for young people with basic skills, preferring to give the technical training themselves. "We'd like to put these kids in an academic program so their skills will improve, but they don't have the skills to survive there," says Otha Myers. "The bottom line is to at least try to make them employable by the time they leave high school."

Voc ed instructors themselves are not all that happy with the situation. They complain that many of the students don't have the basic skills for success in voc ed any more than in English or math. "We've become a dumping ground," says one voc ed instructor. "Students with low verbal and math ability simply cannot grasp the concepts or master the skills necessary for this type of work," says Charlie Adams, who teaches auto mechanics. None of the voc ed faculty has any special experience in dealing with young people with serious learning deficiencies, any more than most of the rest of us do. Voc ed instructors mostly are former tradesmen, mechanics, or chefs—people with solid practical experience and a lot of common sense. But, like the rest of us, they have trouble reaching and motivating kids who lack basic skills and desire.

Their response has been to establish their own system of ability grouping—a voc ed "track system" that is not all that different from the phasing in the English department. On the highest level are students preparing to be "on-line" mechanics, who can handle any repair problem at gas stations or car dealerships. Adams says it takes an IQ of 125 to be effective at such work. On the next level are what Adams calls "manipulative learned skills" (such as repairing brakes) which can be mastered with constant practice. And at the bottom rung of the vocational ladder are such "skills" as "tire busting"—removing a tire from its rim. Adams maintains that students who study auto mechanics gain concrete benefits. He points with pride to the fact that the top twenty percent of his students go on to the Nashville Automotive and Diesel College, then find work as diesel or aircraft mechanics; more than 60 percent of all his students get jobs related to their training.

The controversy about voc ed in high schools is an old and unresolved one. Voc ed is one of the things we got as we tried to make high schools all things to all people. Voc ed's supporters feel that teaching practical skills is a way for a school to meet the needs of one kind of student. The critics argue that these are the wrong skills for schools to be teaching.

"The career wing was a five-million-dollar mistake," says Guidance Director McClure. "We should turn the place into a reading and math center, bring in some specialists, get some innovative approaches, and get serious about educating these kids. They can go to a community college to learn auto mechanics and that stuff."

For all the macho behavior of some of our poorest readers, they're really painfully aware of their inadequacies. One morning, Principal Tony Hanley found a group of kids waiting for the arrival of their teacher, who was late. After Tony let them into the classroom with his key, one of them called out, "Mr. Hanley, please close the door when you go out. People will come by and say, 'That's the class for dummies.'"

What to do? For starters, we could make some headway in literacy by appreciating how fragile the ego and self-esteem of young black people are. A commitment to encourage the many black kids whose potential hasn't been recognized or cultivated could make a difference right away.

In the fall of 1983, I had seven blacks in my three advanced, college-credit English classes. By the end of the year, five of the seven had attempted to drop out. Maybe a couple of them were a little beyond their depth. But the same could be said for at least one-fourth of my white honors students.

My strategy with the blacks was to bend a bit at the start. I could have torn their papers apart with red ink and F's. Instead, I was generous with the praise and usually didn't go below a C-minus in their grades. In the months that followed I was approached at one time or another by all but two with a request to drop the course. I'd laugh it off and simply refuse to consider it. In one case, I went to a girl's counselor and told him not to let her out. By January, the strategy was paying off. One girl, whose papers had been wretched in September, was writing clearly. And another, who'd been writing poorly, was exhibiting some confidence and fluency. When April rolled around, and it was time for my students to sign up for the national English advanced placement test that could qualify students for college credit, I faced another hurdle. Four of my black students didn't sign up. I decided not to fight the decision of three of them. I had my doubts that they could pass and wasn't anxious to have them waste the $49 registration fee and suffer a blow to their self-esteem. But holdout Veda Nicely was a different story. I'd first met her the previous spring when she approached me in the hall.

"You're Mr. Welsh, aren't you?" she asked. "I signed up for your class next year. Do you think I can do the work?"

"Sure," I replied.

From the beginning, she was one of my favorites. An imposing five-foot-eight, she had grown up next to the public housing projects on the east end of town. In that environment, she'd had to overcome the prevailing street ethic, which tore down ambition and academic motivation. "There's great pressure on the kids in the projects not to study," Veda had explained to me. "They call you a 'honkylover' if you work hard in school. They'll go home, throw down the books, and hit the streets. Hanging out is big with them. And you can't blame them. It's almost impossible to study in some homes. There'll be babies crying—children of unmarried sisters. For a lot of these kids, graduating is really a big deal, because their parents didn't. But they don't care if they got all D's, as long as they get to walk."

But Veda persevered. Maybe her physical size prevented her from being intimidated into buying that way of thinking, but I think it was something deeper. Streetwise and physically imposing, Veda looked you straight in the eye and said exactly what was on her mind. The fact that she was only one of three black students in an AP class of thirty-one didn't seem to faze her a bit. When I asked a question or called for a volunteer, her hand was one of the first to go up. Once when she was reading a poem out loud for the class, some wimpy-looking guys began laughing when she stumbled over a word. She paid no attention.

Several months into the school year, the entire class got a demonstration of Veda's character and courage. We were reading Shakespeare's *Othello* when a white guy remarked about the apparent racism of some of the characters. Suddenly Veda blurted out, "Look who's talking about racists— the biggest racist in the school!" There was a tense silence. Not sure what to do, I let it slide and continued with the lesson. But Veda wasn't through with her surprises. At the start of the class next day, she stood up and made a short statement. "I have an apology to make. I was way out of line yesterday when I called Paul a racist. I'm sorry." Once again I was at a loss for words, and tried humor to ease the tension. "That was real white of you, Veda," I said. Everybody laughed and we went back to *Othello*.

Because of the anti-achievement ethic, blacks who take advanced courses often are labeled "Uncle Toms" or "Oreos" (black on the outside, white on the inside). Not Veda. When another black called her a "jelly-butt" in the hall one day, he found himself pushed up against the wall with Veda's menacing fist pressed against his jaw.

When I began telling people around school how much I liked having Veda in class, though, I got some unexpected reactions. "She might disappoint you—wait and see," a counselor cautioned me. Bob Atkins, who coached Veda for the 440 relay and 220 low hurdles, told me, "She's great until you cross her. Watch out." They knew Veda better than I did, but as the year went on she seemed to prove them wrong. Her writing improved dramatically, except for a few spells when, I suspect, she was suffering from normal teen-age blues. Then she stunned me when she broke the news that she wouldn't take the national AP test. No amount of pleading would persuade her to change her mind.

I realized that this was the moment—the test—that Bob and the counselor had warned me about. I enlisted the help of another English teacher, Mary Payne, who knew Veda's mother from church. Veda had been making excuses about not having the $49 fee. Mary said her church group would make it up. Counselor Otha Myers took her aside for a long talk. That did it. Veda gave in. On July 6, the test results of my advanced placement students came back. I looked down the list to find Veda's score. She'd qualified for college credit!

I haven't seen her since she enrolled at George Mason University. I just hope she discovered that she has as much right as anybody else to go after the things she wants. After all, as Woody Allen once said, success often comes down to nothing more than showing up.

The experience of Patty Spenser is still another example of the low expectations that jeopardize black achievement and self-esteem. Patty was a top student by any standard. She reached the quarterfinals of the National Forensic Competition in Chicago, and is now at Amherst College. But Patty told me that her eighth-grade teacher had tried to keep her out of the honors program. As Patty tells it, the teacher advised her that she'd reached her peak. When Patty entered T. C. Williams, the teacher sent a note to our guidance department saying Patty was "not honors material." Patty told me later that if her mother had not fought to keep her in the program, and if a sensitive counselor had not backed her up, she wouldn't be at Amherst today.

I also think of Larry Ward's "near miss." As Larry related it to me later, two of his teachers, both white, tried to talk him out of attending Boston University. It would be "too competitive," they warned him. But Larry graduated from

BU, went on to earn a master's degree at the University of Maryland, and is now a successful businessman.

If teachers can demoralize kids like Larry and Patty, who happened to have strong families behind them, what about other less advantaged black kids? Most end up the way Rudi Jackson almost did. I met Rudi at summer school, where I was teaching a make-up course for kids who'd failed English. I saw right away that he was a very bright kid. He easily grasped plays and novels as diverse as *Henry IV*, *Othello* and *Song of Solomon*. So I was surprised when he told me his future plans were to work at Grand Union. No teacher had ever seriously talked to him about the possibility of college, so Rudi decided his future was at the checkout counter of a national grocery chain. After summer school I got Rudi to talk to Otha Myers. As a result of that, Rudi took a day off from Grand Union to take the SAT exam. His good scores confirmed what I'd suspected: he was college material. Later he entered Norfolk State.

It would be unfair to conclude from our experience that schools are totally failing minority kids, or that the educational programs introduced in the '60s and '70s to help minorities have accomplished nothing. Some improvement is better than none; Headstart and other programs have surely made a difference. But at the present rate of progress, the "realists" may be right: it could be generations before blacks and whites leave high school with an equal chance to make good in life.

Improving the academic outlook of poor minority kids may be the single biggest task facing education. But proving the realists wrong will require something close to a cultural revolution. It certainly won't be accomplished by cosmetic public-relations measures such as requiring football players to maintain a C average. We'll still have athletes who read no better than third-graders. It won't be achieved by allocating funds for every student to take the Preliminary Scholastic Aptitude Test, as our School Board did. We'll still have kids scoring in the lowest percentile. The Alexandria school system has begun to address the problem. Just before school opened in the fall of 1985, Superintendent Peebles released statistics showing the abysmal performance of blacks on national tests. "Until now, Alexandria schools have not faced up to this problem," he acknowledged in a public statement. Peebles declared that improving the achievement of black students would have the highest priority in the year ahead. Among other things, Peebles is supporting a plan that could send specialists into public housing projects to help mothers prepare their children for entering school.

As a teacher, I can only applaud these steps, for we have to confront four unpleasant facts.

1. Blacks in Alexandria are not reaching their potential in the public schools.
2. Neither the schools nor (more important) the community have yet made an all-out commitment to black literacy and achievement.
3. Racial politics—such as the concern of blacks that they will be labeled, stigmatized, and resegregated, and the anxiety of whites that "their" programs could be jeopardized—has stood in the way of reforms.
4. We won't raise reading scores until we raise the hopes of students. As long as kids truly believe that their options are limited to bagging groceries, they won't have any real use for school.

Blacks are understandably wary of "white solutions." No sooner had Peebles issued his pronouncements about tackling the problem when black school board member Lynnwood Campbell voiced skepticism. "It's P.R.," he said. Suspicion of white "help" runs deep. In nearby Montgomery County, Maryland, a Citizens' Minority Relations Monitoring Committee charged that the federally financed special education program was used to funnel black students out of white classrooms. Some black parents felt that white teachers did not understand the "cultural differences" of black kids, which explained the "swift movement of black students into special education tracks."

Blacks who complain about ability grouping and "funneling" have a point. Our present tracking system does serve mainly the middle class. It often cuts the weaker students off from their best source of education and inspiration: other students. Poor students, thrown together, don't learn—at least under present conditions. On the other hand, mixing students together just for the sake of appearances won't work either. It's virtually impossible to challenge the best students when they're sitting next to kids with poor skills and poor attitudes. We have to take ability into account when we group students, but we have to make more of a commitment to those in the lower groups once that's been done.

At T. C. Williams, black and white faculty members alike have always shied away from forthright discussions of black achievement. One black teacher told me she was afraid blacks would "erupt in anger" if white administrators brought up the matter of black performance. So it seldom is brought up in any meaningful way. When our school set up a committee of blacks and whites to discuss tracking, black teachers sat sullenly, or exploded with angry charges that black kids were being deliberately relegated to the lowest tracks. The committee was disbanded after accomplishing almost nothing.

Yet for all the suspicion and resentment, I know that many blacks and whites at T.C. long to look beyond race, in order to get to the roots of this tragedy. Because of the articles I wrote in 1983–84, I was invited to address a meeting of Alexandria English teachers. When I began discussing an upcoming article on the low achievement of black kids, I could feel the tension in the room—or perhaps it was only inside me. I braced for the expected attack: Why was a white teacher writing about a "black problem"? Instead, two black women began talking about the wretched homes from which so many of these kids come. They talked of illegitimate babies who have never known fathers, of the promiscuity of young, unwed black mothers, and of the anger it generates in their children. When the meeting ended, a black psychologist nudged me and said, "If we could have locked everybody in the room for twenty-four hours we could have really gotten down to it."

Even at the height of the civil rights movement, Alexandria's black community saw that desegregation without academic gains would be a hollow victory. In 1971, black city councilman Ira Robinson attacked the school system for "advancing children who cannot read, or who read poorly." He called for the "immediate adoption of a realistic program designed to teach every educable child in Alexandria to read." Black leaders who issued such statements wanted higher standards; they wanted the schools to demand more from black kids. No one is more concerned about the situation than black teachers. Social studies teacher Charlotte Stokes says there have to be radical changes. "We just can't go on with business as usual if we are going to reach these kids. We have to accept as a given that these kids are not learning in the system as it is structured, and then we have to go out and find teaching strategies that *will* reach them."

In the few communities that have made real commitments, the results have been noteworthy. Consider the case of Atlanta. With ninety percent black enrollment, it has the highest concentration of minority pupils in the United

States outside Washington, D.C. In 1980, sixty-nine percent of its students were scoring below the national norm in reading and sixty-seven percent were below in math. Then, in the summer of 1980, the school system launched a crusade to reach the national norms by 1985.

The city mobilized parents, businesses and citizens. Beginning in 1980, tens of thousands of people attended town meetings to discuss raising standards; businesses adopted schools, and by 1983 more than 5,000 adult volunteers were working in the schools, including 1,000 directly involved in tutoring students. A resuscitated Parent-Teachers Association addressed low achievement, health, teen-age pregnancy, and venereal disease. By 1984, Atlanta students had exceeded the norm in math and were only a few points away in reading.

The Atlanta campaign was based on four assumptions: students have to feel that people who are important to them believe in the goal; students have to see evidence that their efforts are worth while; students have to be given a chance to express their views; and students have to be challenged.

The Atlanta school system has advantages that Alexandria and other school districts lack. It has a large, politically powerful, well-established black middle class, and it is relatively homogenous. Atlanta high schools don't have the vast racial, economic, ethnic, and class differences of T.C. But we can learn lessons from Atlanta, and from other models. The Job Corps is a federal program begun during the War on Poverty that takes a no-nonsense approach to education, but at this writing it faces the Reagan administration's ax. When high school graduates test out at the third-grade level, they're put into third-grade reading classes. When they're successful, they're moved ahead. At Job Corps camps around the country, students spend up to four hours a day on reading and math until they've mastered the basics; the rest of the day they learn practical skills such as carpentry, bricklaying and typing.

The Job Corps has a lot of advantages that we lack. It immerses kids in the basics at residential centers far removed from the street culture that exerts such negative influences. But the Job Corps program is based on the belief that changing *attitudes* is as important as drill and practice in the basics. Using veteran Job Corpsmen to carry the message that it isn't cool to be dumb, it attacks the anti-achievement ethic of the newcomers. It uses peer pressure, military-style discipline, and almost daily evaluation of students' progress, based on high tech computer readouts. It utilizes sports programs and extra-curricular activities to stimulate, motivate, and develop self-confidence and self-esteem. The best Job Corps camps have more the spirit of an Israeli kibbutz than of a traditional American high school. And unlike some other federal programs from the War on Poverty, the Job Corps has statistics to prove that it gets significant results.

Obviously, high schools as now constituted can't replicate the conditions of a Job Corps camp. The Job Corps is expensive, and these are not, apparently, times for costly federal programs. But the Job Corps and the Atlanta experiment may have lessons for us. When kids believe they are working toward something that's important to them, miracles can sometimes happen.

This sense of possiblities is what seems to be missing in a lot of Alexandria's black neighborhoods. I don't want to sound like a reactionary, but I've heard enough of my best black students lament the fact that many of their friends "just want to get on welfare" to wonder about the impact of some of the federal aid programs. It's no secret at T.C. that our worst readers and disciplinary problems live in public housing projects.

"They think the street corner's the world" is how one of my black students puts it. He describes a circle of friends who have fatalistically accepted a lifetime of menial employment. "I used to crack on 'em about their jobs and they'd say, yeah, I'm working construction or I'm with the government. They were sweeping floors and living with their moms."

Schools can instill a sense of possibilities. They can help all students identify their unique personal strengths. To that end, we may have to make changes in the traditional school curriculum, which often seems to destroy self-esteem instead of reinforcing it. Too often kids with serious academic disadvantages are forced to play our game. When they either can't or won't fit in, they're labeled as failures, and decide there's not much in it for them. Since pride and high personal expectations go together, schools could use drama, dance, art, and other "right hemisphere" activities to tap the creativity, enthusiasm, and curiosity that are inside every student. The objective would be to lead students from one success to another, instead of imposing the traditional curriculum's notion of what success is. Success on the stage could create the momentum for working toward success in the physics lab. The important thing would be always to work toward building self-esteem and a feeling that progress was possible.

This might mean creating schools within schools, staffed by specially trained teachers who would work closely with individual students for two- or three-year stints. These teachers could provide weak students with a lot of personal attention. And they would be given special time for sharing information with other teachers on the academic progress of students. If it takes incentive pay to build up a corps of dedicated teachers to work with these kids, so be it; such compensation would be far less controversial among teachers than the fashionable idea of merit pay, since teachers understand the great difficulties of working with poor-reading students.

Such schools-within-schools ought to have a measure of independence and self-government; and they ought to exploit one great untapped resource: other students. They could use our often-bored juniors and seniors—the natural models for younger students—to tutor kids in danger of falling far behind. I'm told that no university student in the South American nation of Colombia graduates without teaching a peasant to read. Why not make teaching others a criterion for graduation in our high schools?

But the community has to be a main force behind any such effort. T. C. Williams is now seen as the "white man's school on the hill." It's not so surprising that few black parents show up for parents night, or participate in the Parent-Teachers-Students Association. Yet we won't succeed without the help of black parents, black civic leaders, black activists, black churches, and the business community. The churches launched the civil rights movement, and could be in the forefront of the new effort in education.

"The churches have been too conservative; they have to get involved with the problems of these kids," says William Euille, a former black member of the school board. Only when Alexandria's black youth begin believing that school can help them will the schools begin to make a difference. Eric Lee, a nineteen-year-old dropout, convinced me of that. Eric is pretty tough-looking; he sports Black Muslim headgear, and was into break-dancing with a street group called the Cold Crush Crew. But looks are deceiving. In the fall of 1984 he returned to school and ended up in my class of twelfth-grade Phase 2 students. After a year of living on his own, supporting himself and spending his spare change on parties and go-go joints, Eric decided he wanted more from life. He used the school for all he could get out of it. He got A's in my class, understood *Song of Solomon*, and did well in all but one other class. He planned to enter the army and have the U.S. government finance the rest of his education. Eric has an advantage: he can read competently. But I think his reading skills grew out of an attitude that made acquiring those skills possible.

It's our job to be ready for kids like Eric when *they* are ready. But that may not be enough. If we don't begin to tackle the educational consequences of poverty more boldly, we could tragically jeopardize the great gains of desegregation. The poverty programs are under fire by conservative politicians, who argue that they didn't work, yet they have little concrete to offer in their place other than vague exhortations to "self-help." It's not enough. Some blacks have begun seriously to question what the "dream" of racial togetherness has brought them. If blacks lose faith, the United States may have to endure a new period of racial strife and division.

I already hear blacks saying the unsayable: that black children received a better education *before* schools were desegregated. John Butler, who was assistant principal at Parker-Gray High School before 1971, looks back in anger. "I was afraid when integration came the blacks wouldn't get a fair shake, that white teachers wouldn't understand their needs, and I was right. They got a better education in segregated schools." Much as I respect John Butler, many educators, including many black ones, would disagree. But his words are a warning. Blacks are frustrated and angry. We didn't end the legacy of inequality at the schoolhouse door in the '60s. Now that legacy can only be abolished once and for all *in* the schoolhouse.

5

Differences

It was the annual Senior Skip Day, when members of the graduating class take an unauthorized day off. At school the previous day, word had spread that *the* Skip Day party would be at a townhouse in a staid part of Alexandria's historic Old Town. Now, at ten-thirty in the morning, the mostly white party crowd, already fortified with screwdrivers, mimosas and strawberry daiquiris, was having trouble keeping strangers out. But outside, cars had begun to block the street and a large crowd of mostly black kids was not taking "come back later" for an answer.

Inside the house, the assembled guests were debating what to do. While some favored keeping it restricted, others were feeling guilty about excluding black friends who were mingling with the strangers outside. "Racist" is one of the worst epithets that can be hurled at T. C. Williams. As the crowd grew, a new concern arose that the police would discover the school-day revelry and break it up. "You *can't* turn them away," Cathy Puskar said. Finally, the door was open to anyone who knocked.

The festivities continued to build for the next couple of hours. Most blacks and whites socialized easily. Mixed couples danced to the loud beat from the family stereo, while some kids engaged in "quarters," a drinking game that involves bouncing quarters into a glass of beer. The only group that was acting left out was what one of our black football stars called "the raw crew"—a black clique whose members are distinguished by their heavy work boots, leather jackets, rag wool hats and "Philly" haircuts with shaved sides and high flat tops. The raw crew attempts to project what one student called a "hard-cool look." On this day, members of the raw crew stationed themselves along walls and up the stairs, from where they dispensed their tough looks and rude comments to passing females, black or white.

By noon, Cathy Puskar had worked up what she later was to call "a good, strong social buzz." It was then that the "locket snatcher" incident occurred. As Cathy went upstairs to check on things—despite her buzz, she still felt responsible for helping her friend, the hostess, keep things orderly—she peeked into the master bedroom and saw a member of the raw crew stuffing a handful of jewelry into his pocket. Emboldened by several strawberry daiquiris, she confronted him.

"What the ——— are you doing here?" she shouted.

"Aw, baby, I ain't doin' nothin'."

"What do you mean, you're stealing her mother's jewelry."

"It ain't nothin' but a little locket, baby. Let me talk to you." The intruder tried to put his arm around Cathy, who grabbed the jewelry out of his pocket and started shouting, "Get out of here." He retreated hastily and rejoined his friends downstairs.

The party continued smoothly until after one o'clock, when somebody suddenly turned the music off and began screaming for everyone to leave. It turned out that the locket snatcher had caused a major ruckus by punching two white girls who had refused his advances. Now a potentially far more serious incident was in the making on the street outside, where the troublesome snatcher was surrounded by a crowd of angry whites and blacks. Chucky Grimes, a black football player who moves easily in white or black circles, was having a heart-to-heart discussion with the snatcher, trying to calm him down. Eric Quinto, our black all-state defensive end, who'd come to T.C. two years earlier from the Bronx, where he learned the game playing tackle football in the streets, was telling Adele Fletcher, "You people shouldn't have let those 'niggers' in. You didn't know them."

Finally, the snatcher got into a car and was driven off—by a *white* girl.

Police arrived a few minutes later, but left after Adele Fletcher, who knew the officers, assured them everything was under control.

At this point, a mixed group of blacks and whites drifted off to a new party at a home in another residential, predominantly-white neighborhood. There the mood was mellow. The black football players acted as hosts, greeting guests, mixing drinks, and inviting the girls to dance to the music of Steel Pulse and Madonna, while some of the preppy white guys complained that the girls wouldn't let them play "their music"—a Lynyrd Skynyrd album. The party broke up in late afternoon.

The next day, as girls reviewed the events of Skip Day, they agreed that the black football players had been the stars of the occasion. "They know how to have fun; they can adapt themselves to an entirely new situation," Brande Stellings was to say later.

"Most white guys just stand around dipping (chewing tobacco)—or they just sit and drink and play that 'get stoned' music you can't dance to," one of her friends complained. "They say, 'Let's get f—— up and crank the Skynyrd.' Then they play it over and over again!"

Although blacks have attended publicly financed schools in Alexandria since 1871, blacks did not go to school with whites until February 1959. Until then, Superintendent

T. C. Williams presided over a segregated school system run along the paternalistic lines of a southern plantation. White school authorities doled out whatever money they saw fit to support a few black schools, and when fourteen black children applied for admission to a white grammar school in August 1958, they were turned away. Soon afterward, Williams attempted to dismiss a black school cafeteria worker who was the mother of one of the fourteen. Williams reinstated her after reports that the Justice Department was looking into civil rights violations, and a federal judge ordered the city to stop making school assignments on the basis of race. But the process of desegregation moved slowly in Alexandria, as Virginia continued its "massive resistance" to the 1954 Supreme Court decision banning segregated schools.

Beginning in September 1959, "Negro" students could apply to the school superintendent in writing to attend a white school in their neighborhood. However, an "ability" test was required and had to be sent to a board in Virginia for approval before admittance could be granted. Not until T. C. Williams High School opened in 1965 did Alexandria abandon this "dual" school system. T.C. became one of three integrated high schools serving the community, but the schools were still far from racially "balanced." At T.C., blacks made up about twelve percent of the student body; at George Washington, it was closer to twenty-five percent; and at "white" Hammond High School in Alexandria's affluent West End, there were just six blacks among 2,169 students. It was not until the fall of 1971, after concern spread that the federal government would impose a plan to reach racial balance in the schools, that real racial balance was achieved in the secondary schools. All the city's eleventh and twelfth graders were sent to T. C. Williams, while the ninth and tenth graders were sent to Hammond and George Washington. That caused such turmoil that the school board decided to wait two more years to achieve racial balance in middle and elementary schools through reorganization and busing. In 1977, T.C. became a three-year high school that served an increasingly diverse mix of races, ethnic groups, nationalities, and economic classes.

Alexandria's attachment to the politics and culture of the South, and its long resistance to integration, made this transition a difficult one. Opposition along the way was "hostile and vicious, as well as vocal," wrote Mark Howard, who chronicled the history of Alexandria desegregation in a 1976 Ph.D. thesis. The desegregation in 1971 of all-white Hammond (which became a junior high school) set off fighting and rock throwing among students. Racial incidents, including cases of arson, continued through the fall.

Since then, violent racial confrontations of the kind that made news headlines have ended. T.C. has become a model of school integration. Today we are educating about an equal number of blacks and whites, along with over 350 foreign students. A sign of our diversity is the fact that we have four teachers assigned full-time to teaching English as a second language. The reactionaries were wrong: integration did not bring the collapse of the Alexandria school system. But a dozen years after racial balance was achieved, Alexandria is still struggling with the aftermath of those events. We know that our very survival as a "quality" high school enjoying the support of middle-class families depends on our ability to maintain harmony. Creating harmony and achieving equity in a universe as diverse as ours requires the constant, unrelenting, patient effort of every administrator, teacher, and coach. It is harder and more frustrating work than most of the public knows.

Integration vastly broadened the options available to all kids. It gave them the chance to be more than "black," or

"white"—not to mention "Oriental," "poor," or "prep"—
and to express their individuality beyond those labels. But it
never guaranteed that they would take advantage of the opportunity. A lot of our students still cling to "their group,"
still judge each other on the basis of appearance, still put
much stock in labels, and, sadly, still miss out on the personal growth that can come from really knowing those who
are "different."

The social separateness of races, classes, and ethnic groups
is something of a disappointment to liberals who had high
hopes that integration would happen quickly. "It's disap-
pointing that my daughter has hardly any black friends,"
said Jacqueline Berkman, whose daughter Kathy was in my
English class in 1983–84. When Mrs. Berkman entered Baltimore's Western High in the late '50s, her black friends
could eat only at "colored" restaurants, and suffered other
forms of blatant discrimination. Berkman joined the Congress of Racial Equality and became active in civil rights.
Now she says, "It's ironic; I spent nights in jail with black
friends after sit-ins. Now my daughter goes to a school that
has as many blacks as whites, but almost all her friends are
middle-class whites." Her feelings are echoed by Linda Pe-
terson, who deliberately moved to Alexandria so her son
could be in an integrated school. "It just hasn't worked out
the way we thought it would. Almost all his friends are
white."

But this isn't really so surprising. Kids arrive at high
school when their need to be accepted by their peers can be
at odds with their struggle to establish an identity of their
own. Left to their own devices, kids tend toward conformity,
by race, class, ethnic group, nationality, dress—even musical tastes. Racism isn't the only kind of prejudice that's at
work at T.C. The reality is that on all levels, and in every
racial, economic, nationality, and gender group there's still

plenty of irrational prejudice and just plain nastiness toward "those others."

There's the subtle prejudice that middle-class white kids reveal when a black outdoes them on some academic test. "It couldn't have been *her* that got one of the highest scores," I overheard a white student say about an American history advanced placement test. But it was "her." There's plenty of black racism, too. "Get out of my way, white-ass bitch." "Get out of my mirror, bitch." "I'm gonna step on your face, whitie." "Hey, blondie, why are you so cold?" "Your white hair smells so funny." So goes the hall and bathroom banter on a normal day. Coming to school on the bus, black guys will stretch out over an entire seat, refusing to let white kids sit down. Most of the time, it's more teasing and taunting than threatening. But at its worst, black racism takes the more sadistic form of "ripping off" possessions of affluent whites.

It's ironic, if logical, that the familiar old yellow school bus—symbol of desegregation—is often the neutral territory where real racial biases are expressed and acted out. In recent years, whites coming from Old Town and downtown ran to get on what they called "the white bus," while blacks filled up another bus on the same route and harassed any tardy white kid who boarded it. Students tell me one reason so many of them drive cars to school is that the behavior on the buses is so bad. All kids try to ride on buses operated by black male drivers, who, they say, keep order better than "those redneck women drivers."

Within the white student body, there's the clash of class. A preppy wouldn't be caught dead hanging around with a "grit," a type that dresses down in T-shirts and jeans. Then there's the way established white preppies look down on Afghan refugee kids because of their "tight shirts, polyester pants, and shiny footwear," as a Vietnamese girl familiar with both groups described it. When they're not putting each other down, blacks and whites often turn their prejudices against foreigners. "Whites are just not friendly, and some blacks are real mean to us," says Narong Mookbanditpong. "The blacks call me Chin-Chong the Chink, and I'm not even Chinese. I'm Thai!"

"The other day in the library some black guy comes up to me and screams to his friends, 'Hey, look at the Chinese vampire.' It made me angry. They don't seem to like oriental people." So complains a Taiwanese.

"The American students are so cold to us, they don't like to talk to us," says Zaher Zaher, an Afghan student. "When I first left Afghanistan, I went to school in Rome. The Italian students were so warm. They reached out to the foreign students, even those like me who could hardly speak Italian. After two months in Rome I had so many Italian friends I couldn't believe it. After a year and a half here, I only have one close American friend, a black guy I work with at McDonald's."

"Weren't all Americans just foreigners once? Didn't they all come from somewhere else?" says a girl from Bangladesh. "Why are they so mean to us?" These students often speak in halting English, but they have no trouble describing the callous intolerance that sometimes confronts foreign students at T. C. Williams.

"It just pains me so to hear my son complain about the foreign kids all sitting together and 'jabbering' in their native languages," says the mother of a white student in my class. "I tell him that when his grandfather was in high school in North Dakota, students mocked him for his heavy Norwegian accent, but it just doesn't seem to sink in."

A casual glance around the T. C. Williams cafeteria at lunchtime reveals the way students cling to their own. At a large round table, ten dark-haired Afghans converse in their own language. At one end of a long adjacent table are several Orientals. At the other end half a dozen white girls from the crew surround a preppy white guy sporting a pink-striped button-down shirt. Nearby are the "freaks"—kids with punk hair styles and New Wave clothes. Although the blacks keep to their own tables, an expert eye can quickly sort out the subgroups: the basketball team, the Del Ray crew (named for an Alexandria neighborhood), the West End girls, and the "town boys" from the housing projects in Old Town. We have esoteric cliques such as the Skoal Dippers, who've formed around the "sport" of spitting chewing tobacco.

Dress imposes its own social definitions. "There are just three things you need to be accepted as an 'in' sophomore girl: Guess jeans, Esprit blouses, and Mia shoes," a girl told me. Minh Vu, '85, a Vietnamese girl in my honors course, learned this the hard way. "My first year in junior high school was a disaster. Even though I'd been in the U.S. five years, I dressed like I'd just come off the boat. I could kill my parents for not knowing how to dress me 'properly.' But in eighth-grade I caught on. I became the epitome of prep and was finally accepted. If you dress badly, they're merciless!" Minh says a couple of Afghan and Oriental girlfriends do date American guys, "but they're not the preppy, conservative types."

Sometimes you'd hardly know legal segregation in Alexandria ended twenty years ago. In the last twelve years only four whites have been on the basketball team. But there are only two black girls on our varsity crew. Anybody who watched our crew races would think we were a preppy, white private school. For some reason, few blacks play baseball, and whites are becoming an unusual sight on the football field. There were five on the forty-five roster of our championship '84–85 team.

When I first came to T.C. there was only one black cheer-

leader, and the athletic department was under pressure to re-
cruit more. Now the pendulum has swung the other way.
Once black girls made the cheerleading squad, the white
girls seemed to retreat. By the fall of '84, there was only one.

The school system to some degree reinforces these cultural groupings. From third grade on, it sorts, tracks and
groups students by academic ability. Special programs such
as vocational education and remedial reading fill up quickly
with mostly black kids, while whites dominate the "gifted
and talented" program. It isn't just kids who stereotype kids.
We do it, too. "They just thought I was a dumb nigger because I used to fight a lot," a black honors student told me.
"Accidentally they looked at my records and found I was
pretty smart, so they moved me. I wonder how many other
misplaced blacks are just rotting in those classes."

Academically, it makes sense to group kids by ability,
even when in doing so, classrooms can become "segregated"
again. I cannot, as a teacher, think what else we could do.
Where we're failing, in my opinion, is in being passive in the
face of students' natural tendency to stick to their own.
There's no reason white kids can't play football, or blacks
can't row. T.C.'s 1971 state championship football team—
voted the best high school team in the history of the Washington metropolitan area by local coaches and sportswrit-
ers—was half white. We haven't done enough to discourage
racial retreats from, or takeovers of, sports and extracurricular activities. In short, we haven't done enough to give integration a helping hand.

Still, even without that extra push, centuries-old social
conventions are breaking down. In some cases, we're witnessing a reversal of the stereotypes. Consider the complaints of Thornton Walker, a six-foot-one, 210-pound
linebacker in the class of '85. Thornton is a shy, quiet, handsome black guy not given to flirting with girls. But after the

team's big '84 season, Walker was often embarrassed by the direct approach of upper-middle-class white girls, who, he complains, furtively pinched him and made lewd remarks.

Wide receiver Chucky Grimes has had similar experiences. "I always wanted to do that," one Old Town white girl told him after administering one such grab. "You look so nice in your tight football pants." Chucky is mildly amused. "These aren't redneck white trash," he says. "They're upperclass!"

Mark Moore, who started in the Alexandria school system in kindergarten in 1971—the year the final stage of desegregation began—has had his ups and downs mixing with white kids in the school system. Mark's mother associated with whites at work and had white friends to her house, Mark recalls. He himself remembers walking to school with whites for the first few years of grammar school and playing with them after school. In junior high, he curtailed his socializing with whites and hung out mostly with his black friends, "playing basketball and chasing girls." By the middle of eleventh grade, however, he found himself mixing with white kids again, attending parties and hanging around with them at sports events.

In the fall of senior year, Mark became friends with Brande Stellings, a white classmate. Brande, who came from what she describes as a lower-middle-class home, had just transferred to T.C. from the nation's most prestigious private boarding school, Phillips Exeter Academy, which she'd attended on scholarship. She and Mark got to know each other working at a movie theater after school a few evenings a week. Through Brande, Mark began getting invitations to weekend parties of Brande's white friends. It wasn't long before Mark was moving with the "in" white crowd.

Of the white girls he's met, Mark says, "I'm willing to be friends and leave it at that. It's enough. It's exciting." He was one of the guests at the Skip Day party that broke up after the incidents. "That black guy ruined things for the rest of us," he said. "We were afraid that the whites would have the general impression that all black guys were like that. But they didn't or they wouldn't have invited me and my friends to the second party."

Mark knows he's breaking new ground. In general, the parents of his white friends "have been accepting," though he remembers some "double takes" from an Old Town mother when her daughter brought him home. "It's better if the parent knows ahead," Mark says. "I got this look that said, 'I didn't know he was *black*.' But eventually she warmed up to me."

This kind of mixing is clearly changing the old rules of the game and causing some new social tensions. "The white guys seem to shy up when we come around to the parties," I was told by Shawn McNeil, a black star on the football team. McNeil says, however, that the white guys aren't nearly so perturbed as some black girls, who've gone on the warpath. "They're getting seriously upset," Mark Moore acknowledged, "They don't like us talking to what they call 'our little white friends.' "

A lot of black kids say that they're more willing to "cross over"—and are more at ease when they do—than whites. "We go to their parties and aren't nervous. It's just a party to us. But when my sister had a surprise party for me and invited white friends, they seemed really nervous at first and weren't sure they wanted to be there," Chucky Grimes says.

But some white kids *are* crossing over. John Vaughn, a brawny guy who's half American and half Japanese, is disappointed more whites don't come out for football. When John began playing football in a grammar school recreation league, older black kids would come to games and taunt the white players. He was intimidated enough to quit, but in eighth grade he and a bunch of whites got together and went out for the junior high school team. Another who went out was Mike Porterfield, who said, "Once the black guys saw we were good they accepted us." As it turned out, both starred on the offensive line of the '84 team.

John acknowledges that being big helped. But irrational fears and the attitudes that go with them, not size, are what keeps most whites away from football, John believes. Whites, he says, are afraid to go to summer football camp, where those trying out live together in a college dorm for two weeks. They just don't want to be in a situation where *they* are the minority, he says. But staying the course has been rewarding. In eleventh grade, both John and Mike finally felt they were accepted. The big moment came when they were subjected to the traditional initiation rite of being sprayed with skin-burning ointment in the locker room.

During the last couple of seasons, John and Mike found out what it was like to be on the receiving end of racial slurs. In games against suburban teams with predominantly white rosters, they were often taunted as "niggers" along with their black teammates as they lined up for plays. John and Mike took particular pleasure in opening up holes for our black running backs, and grinding down the racists on the opposite side of the line. Now they both feel there's a real bond with their black teammates. Black players call John "Heiko" (his Japanese mother's name), and Mike often slips into black dialect when he gets together with his teammates.

As a football player, a black can cultivate white friends without losing status among blacks. It isn't always so easy for blacks who are succeeding in other areas. Dirck Hargraves and Patty Spencer, both black, are examples of that. Dirck was president of the senior class in 1983–84; Patty was vice-president of student government.

"In grammar school, I was in the gifted and talented program," Dirck told me. "All my classmates were white, but I never noticed color then. It wasn't until seventh grade that I was aware of the rift between the races. It was a nightmare, because I felt I didn't fit into either group. The black guys made life miserable for me. They mocked me about my preppy clothes, my white friends, the fact that I didn't talk street lingo, the fact that I didn't like to fight. They were always calling me Oreo. For a while the white kids were my refuge, but then I realized that though they were nice to me, they really didn't accept me. They singled me out as something different, as if I wasn't really black because I was so smart."

Through fifth grade, Patty Spencer attended Washington private schools. "All the black kids were middle class; they thought just like I did; they were serious about school. But when I entered the Alexandria schools in sixth grade, I was shocked to see that so many of the black students didn't care about education. I got incredible hostility from them. They mocked me about the way I talked, about my liking to read, about everything they could. I immediately got this snobbish bookworm image that even to this day I haven't been able to shake. There were many days when I went home in tears because of what some black kid said or did."

Patty was put in the gifted and talented program, where most of her classmates were white. "On the surface the white kids have been nice to me, but the racism of a lot of them, especially the boys, is outrageous. I don't know whether they forget that I'm black or if they do it on purpose, but I've been with groups of white kids who'll start describing black kids as 'niggers' and suddenly say, 'Oh, we don't mean you; please don't be offended.' Or they'll start imitating what they think is black speech—that Amos and Andy stuff—without any idea of how hurtful it is. Right now they're saying I'll only get into good colleges because I'm black."

Riding through Alexandria with white classmates, Dirck recalls feeling like the invisible man. "They'd look at blacks on the streets and call them niggers, as if I wasn't there." His father helped pull him through when the going got rough. "I remember asking my dad why blacks had to put down one of their own who tried to be successful. 'Jewish people helped each other, didn't they? Why can't blacks?' I asked him. He told me it wasn't really the black kids' fault; the environment they came from was a creation of white racism. He said whites had done a divide-and-conquer routine on us, turning the nonachievers who have been destroyed by racism against the achievers.

"That advice helped a lot, but what helped most was when I suddenly said to myself, 'I'm just going to be myself, and the hell with what anybody, black or white, thinks of me.'"

In band, they still chuckle about the Canadian.

"Are blacks and whites forced to sit separately on your buses?" he had asked when the T.C. school band arrived in Ottawa for a musical competition. One bus was filled mostly with blacks, the other with whites.

Donald Hill, a black saxophonist, says he usually sits with black kids on long band trips. But race isn't the reason. It's because of the "funk" music he knows his black friends will be playing on tapes. "Music is the thing on the buses, more than race," says Donald. "The white kids will be listening to jazz or rock. But just because we sit separately on those long trips doesn't mean we're not close. We're a real tight group. Because of the band I have a lot of white friends. In fact, if it weren't for band I don't think I'd really know many white kids at all."

"I used to be afraid of blacks," trumpet player Joe Isaja told me. "I thought I was going to have to fight them all the time. From the band, I now have all kinds of black friends and I realize how crazy my thinking was. The band has made me much more social. It's given me an incredible range of friends. We're all drawn together by the music, and then get to know each other. Suddenly it's no longer preppy, or grit, black or white, it's 'band person.' "

The Canadian story convinces me that if racial concerns didn't exist we'd probably have to invent them. When a black guy hassles a white female in the halls, the white assumes it's race. But it isn't—not always. It may be class. And it may be *teen-age*.

A white girl told me once how annoying the racial harassment from black guys was. "Hey, baby; hey, shortie, that kind of stuff. They'll grab my arm or try to block my way, then start saying those offensive things. It doesn't scare me but I shouldn't have to put up with it. The worst part about it is that it gives the girls it happens to a bad feeling about black guys. Then we go home and feel guilty because our liberal parents are obsessed that their children should have only nice feelings about blacks."

"My parents keep asking me when I'm going to bring a black guy home," adds another senior. "But what they really want is some nice Oreo on his way to Harvard. Even when I come back from school mad because some black guy has pinched my rear end, they tell me that I should try to understand. 'He hasn't had the same background as you.' "

These girls are struggling against feeling "antiblack." But if they talked to black girls they'd hear many of the same complaints about the behavior of some black males. "Those guys did that to me until I threatened to get my boyfriend after them," I was told by Cassandra Menefee, a black senior in the class of '84. "They didn't mess with me after they found out I went with *Dexter!*"

For some, this school can be a difficult, even a painful place. The tensions and conflicts aren't always beneficial. Sometimes they leave scars: bad memories of other races and classes that won't be erased in a lifetime. Some kids really might be better off in a smaller, more homogeneous school.

But it works the other way, too. Cathy Ribble, for example, transferred to T.C. from a local private school at the beginning of tenth grade. Two years later, she's ecstatic about that decision. At private school, there were only fifty in her class, and she felt she couldn't fit in with any group. They told her that if she switched to T.C., she'd be knifed in the halls, beaten up in the parking lot, and forced to take drugs. But it didn't work out that way.

"At private school you had to have your clothes down right. In eighth grade, they had rainbows of alligator shirts. When *The Washington Post* said alligator was out everyone bought polos. I went out and bought all these preppy clothes before I came to T.C., so I'd be accepted. But when I walked in and saw all different kinds of kids and styles of dress, I realized I could be what I wanted."

Months after it happened, I still kept seeing a scene from the 1984 Virginia AAA state championship game between T.C.'s Titans and Hampton High School. It was early in the third quarter and though we had a 10–0 lead, the more than 2,000 T.C. fans who made the drive to the University of Virginia's stadium in Charlottesville were getting nervous. Hampton was proving much tougher than expected. Members of the school board, the superintendent, and various groups of middle-aged, preppy-looking parents were seated halfway up the stadium seats at the fifty-yard line. I was just to their left, struggling to keep my two-year-old Claire from running down the steps. Way down on the bottom row, closer to the field, were forty or fifty tough-looking T.C. black guys with leather jackets and "Philly" haircuts—members of the raw crew. They'd been moving up and down the field to keep even with the ball.

Suddenly Shawn McNeil fielded a Hampton punt on our thirty-five-yard line, broke three tackles, and exploded up the middle of the field. The whole T.C. crowd rose to its feet screaming, "Go, Shawn, go!" And the raw crew rolled down the sidelines with him like a wave. Shawn went forty yards before being tackled.

For the five or six seconds of McNeil's run and for a few heady moments afterward, it suddenly felt as if T.C. was one school. I knew that on Monday morning, when the excitement began to wear off, kids would retreat to their groups and the dignitaries on the fifty-yard line would feel safer if they never had to see a member of the raw crew in their neighborhood. T.C. would go back to its racial separation, its cliquishness, its class snobbery. We have not reached and probably never will reach the ideal of being one community. And still, I'm convinced that the school's diversity is one of its great assets. Kids are getting a realistic understanding of the "others," even if real integration, we know now, will take longer than we'd hoped twenty years ago. For the majority of kids, the years at T.C. are the only time in their lives they're exposed in anything but a superficial way to the people they share this country with. This is a profound education in its own right. And it's this education that many T.C. graduates hold on to long after they've forgotten the classroom lessons we taught them.

For blacks, learning to feel at ease with whites is more than a matter of enrichment. It's essential to their success or failure in life. For better or worse, America is still a white-dominated society, a country in which the way up inevitably leads out into the white world. T.C. is a place for learning to cope with this reality. It takes courage and toughness to fight the peer pressure and break away from one's own. Those who succeed testify that it's worth it.

Everett Ward, who describes himself as coming from a "lower-middle-class family in Alexandria's south side," is one of those. When he arrived at an Ivy League college after graduating from T.C., he found the transition to a place that was 90 percent white "very easy." Today, he's finishing up at Harvard Law School.

For whites, the experience has its own special value. "My life is so much richer because of the black friends I made through football," says Mike Sharkey, a white who has since graduated from Georgetown University Medical School. "If I hadn't gotten to know these guys I'd be so ignorant about people, about American society, about life in general. I know I'll be a better doctor because of all the different types of people I got to know in high school. Kids who don't get that kind of experience are really missing something."

6

The Fifty-Minute Year

"The minutes tick by slowly on the clock. The big hand moves toward the one. Fifteen minutes more to go. One, two, three . . . eighty-two, eighty-three, eighty-four. Imagine that, I think, eighty-four tiles in the ceiling. I wonder how many there are in the floor. I look out the window and then glance again at the clock. Ten more minutes left. I doodle, stop, and begin again. As I glance up, the teacher looks at me and asks a question. 'Yes,' I say. 'I'm paying attention.' Of course I know the answer. This is the third time we have done this problem. I look at the clock yet again and see that only five minutes remain. A friend passes me a note. I read it, respond, and pass it back. I take a piece of gum out of my purse and begin to chew it slowly. The bell rings, signaling the end of class."

This is Anne Marie Cushmac, class of '85, National Merit Scholar, recipient of an early acceptance to the University of Virginia, writing about a day in school.

Betsy Yoder writes, "The thought of writing on boredom excited me. Because it's mine! I understand it, and I hate it. And because I'd finally get to tell someone, and maybe they'd listen."

Cassandra Johnson comments: "The ennui in school causes me to hate the thing I love the most—art. When in class, the drawing and painting means tedious exercises or chores. Whereas it is at home that I do my best work, or at least enjoy what I am doing."

111

Paul Swanson writes, "There is no feeling [at school] that more than physical presence is required."

Cathy Puskar puts it bluntly: "In a school of over 2,000 students, it is only a select group of some 300, maybe, that are interested in and, enjoying, some aspect of school other than the purely social aspect."

It's unsettling to learn from students that their most rewarding moments don't come in my English class but making hamburgers at Roy Rogers, "pumping iron" in the weight room, rehearsing for a play, or tutoring a mentally retarded child. It's easy to shrug this off and just blame the kids. Haven't most kids *always* found schools boring? Didn't *we* find it so? If they weren't in school, where *would* they be? Doesn't our school offer more courses and stimulating outside activities than most? Why blame the school?

But I think we should listen carefully to the message students are sending us. We're in a struggle for the attention of our children, and we're losing it. We're losing out to the distractions of electronic media, part-time jobs, and an affluent, seductive youth culture. But by paying close attention to what it is that *does* excite and interest young people, we just might get important clues about how to make schools more inspiring, exciting, and useful. We can ask ourselves what needs of school children are *not* being satisfied by television or the youth culture, and what they are finding at after-school jobs or tutorial programs for retarded youngsters that is absent in their classrooms. Once we understand the answers to those questions, we can, perhaps, begin recasting lesson plans, the school day, curriculums, and our overall objectives to fit the changed conditions of the '80s and '90s.

We still have something very important going for us. Kids still love coming to school!

Soon after seven o'clock every morning, school buses begin pulling up in front of the building, and out pour throngs of young people who look anything but bored. The energy of this multitude infects even an aging English teacher. It's a reminder that young people want to be with other young people, and school is where it happens. A group of black football players are bunched together while some shy girls try to nudge their way into the conversation. The cliques are beginning to show their colors. A bunch of "ultimate preppy" girls are gossiping their heads off. The Skoal Dippers (tobacco chewers) are gathering. (The dippers used to carry plastic cups around with them as portable spittoons, but since tobacco stains were found on the rugs in the library they've been forbidden to practic their art in the building.) Also arriving are "grits," distinguishable by their uniform: jean jackets over white T-shirts. As people move slowly toward classrooms, the talk continues about weekend parties, new dating arrangements, and recent trades by the Baltimore Orioles.

But all too often, when the bell rings at seven-thirty, the spontaneity, energy, and enthusiasm evaporate. Order reigns. The corridors are empty and silent. The stylized game of school has begun. The students pretend to be paying attention—even to be interested. They take tests, get their grades, and finally receive their diplomas. And we cover the material, keep our students "on task," and complete the "objectives of the lesson plan." Sometimes we're taken in ourselves. Because we are talking and active, we mistakenly assume that we're stimulating something in the minds of kids. But in the last couple of years, I've begun to feel that these kids tolerate hours of boredom and trivial routine almost as a favor to us.

Schools have an obsession with time. There's a compulsion to program and control every minute of the day—ironic when one considers that hours can be wasted on bored students. One of the best-loved clichés of administrators is "time on task." Some insightful pedagogue at some school of education had concluded that the number of minutes a student spends on a particular assignment has a direct bearing on how well he or she learns it. School bureaucracies all over the country are now attempting to translate this revelation into all kinds of rules and regulations.

One educational consultant advising the Alexandria schools devised a way to soak up the "wasted" time at the start of each new class. A "sponge activity"—a brief assignment to be scrawled on the blackboard—would focus the attention of newly arrived students before they could relax or start a conversation with a classmate. This "innovation" reflected the current anxiety in education circles that too many precious minutes which students could be spending "on task" are being squandered.

Teaching methods that give us such things as the sponge activity are in an old tradition of schooling that holds that "the quiet child is the good child." The trouble with this thinking is that it can destroy the spontaneity that makes school exciting. The goal seems to be a risk-free environment—one in which classes never get out of hand, subjects taught do not threaten or offend students, and grading is "in line" with normal curves.

But risk and spontaneity are at the *heart* of learning! The best moments in my class are frequently those that are totally unprepared—when, for one reason or another, my students take me in an unexpected direction. As teachers, we instinctively want to pull back, but it's important to resist that urge. I remember a class in early 1985 when we drifted away from the planned discussion of the plot and character development in *Portrait of the Artist* while my students engaged in a heated and completely unplanned debate about the meaning of a young girl's "giving her gift." The battle raged for ten minutes, with several girls saying the "gift" was her body while the boys argued for another interpretation. I could feel my trained teacherly reflexes telling me to get back to the material, even though it was obvious the digression was getting the whole class involved.

I want my class to be fun. A sense of humor is one of a teacher's greatest assets. But you won't find the new literature on "effective teaching" dwelling much on the need for fun and spontaneity in classrooms. I don't dictate "notes," as many teachers do. Students who silently scribble away with their faces in their books and papers drive me up the wall. The longer I teach, the more determined I am to combat passivity. Sometimes I stop where I am and just say, "Write off the top of your heads for ten minutes on the poem we've been discussing."

Teaching often involves an element of trickery—the purpose being to "trick" kids into suspending the "game" long enough to let their natural curiosity and enthusiasm come out. On first reading, many of my honor students find Joyce's short story "The Boarding House" excruciatingly dull. It's about a thirty-five-year-old man who gets roped into a loveless marriage by a conniving younger woman. "What's boring about sexual blackmail?" I ask the kids. "Isn't that why most people get married?" Often within minutes we're into an intense debate about male-female relationships and the story comes to life.

Nobody knows how to fight passivity and boredom better than T.C.'s brilliant chemistry teacher, John Liebermann. John can uncover interest in kids where other teachers fail. Several years ago he had a boy who was bright but bored. John heard that the boy liked photography, so he devised a science project that would put this interest to work. John casually suggested that an interesting experiment would be to use a camera to discover the amount of iron in a vitamin tablet. The boy would photograph an electric arc passing through the tablet, develop the pictures, and use the changes in the light to figure the amount of iron present. The boy was intrigued. He caught fire. At the University of Rochester he majored in chemistry.

Liebermann does not get extra effort from kids by bribing them with higher grades, or other special recognition, either. In the winter of 1985, seven of John's students won awards in the annual Westinghouse Science Talent Search Project. (T.C. had the fourth largest number of semifinalists in the whole country, after The Bronx High School of Science, Stuyvesant, and Benjamin N. Cardozo—all of whose students are pre-selected for their academic ability.) Our winners were intelligent kids, but not necessarily brilliant scientists. They won by hard work—thousands of hours spent after school or on weekends—sometimes until eight o'clock. What was remarkable about this was that John gave no extra credit for the work, and, of course, there was no guarantee that all those hours would result in prizes.

What the kids get out of the experience is no mystery. It's a strongly positive sense of owning one's own education, of learning through doing, of discovery for its own sake and of sharing with others the pride of hard work.

In February 1985, the African Heritage Dancers and Drummers performed at a school assembly. Other than sports contests, which occur in the relative safety of the gym or the great outdoors, we don't have too many events that bring the whole school together in one confined place. The school administration is always nervous about these assemblies. The concern is that troublemakers could cause an incident, and the "image" of T.C. could suffer.

Melvin Deal, director of the African Heritage group, is an imposing, six-foot-four black man who, on the appointed day, appeared on stage wearing an African headdress. The sight immediately inspired giggling and snickering from the crowd of 1,600 kids. As the noise continued, Deal stared out at the audience, his hands folded across his chest.

"I don't talk while fools are talking," he intoned patiently after things finally settled down. He looked over at a section of the audience where the noise had been coming from, and addressed those students. "Blacks are going to have to decide whether they're going to be a cartoon in American life, or part of the mainstream."

Silence. Some wiseguy laughed.

"You think everything's a big joke," Deal went on. "You're not going to think it's a joke when you're out there with no skills and can't get a job. I know that ninety percent of you are serious, but it only takes the ten percent of the rest of you to ruin everything."

This time a girl couldn't contain her giggling.

"You'll think it's funny next year when you're unemployed, pregnant and the father's disappeared."

Silence. Utter silence.

This sobering introduction over, Deal was ready to begin. He congratulated the rest of the audience for its cooperation and began talking about the origin of West African dance. His musical group played while he taught the audience a chant. He invited students to come forward and learn a Senegalese dance. Several dozen volunteers rush to the stage. He called for half a dozen teachers to join in. He explained that break-dancing was derived from West African acrobatic dancing, and invited break-dancers from the T.C. student body to show off their skills on stage. Six boys and two girls performed. Two of the boys were plainly more skillful than Deal's own break-dancers, and the audience loved it. Deal chanted to the accompaniment of his drum. One of the best assemblies we've ever had ended.

As I walked out of the auditorium, I wanted Melvin Deal

to become assistant principal of T. C. Williams High on the spot. I wanted him to help us motivate kids. I wished that every class could have the same intensity and excitement that was present in that assembly. And I wanted him to give all of us the courage to speak unpleasant truths to teen-agers.

Deal had demonstrated that taking risks can pay off. But risk-taking is not, evidently, on the agenda of the people who are now busily attempting to reform high schools. In the summer of 1983, in an effort to put more rigor into the curriculum, the Virginia Department of Education announced that all students would have to take two full years of a laboratory science instead of one. Half-year courses would no longer count as a credit toward high school graduation. As a result, T.C. completely dropped three of the most popular elective courses in the school—acoustics, botany and microbiology—and announced that oceanography and astronomy would be offered only every other year. The state wanted to strengthen science education by requiring more mastery of the basics and eliminating "frills." But in the opinion of our science department, the effect was exactly the opposite. The planetarium, always popular with our budding scientists, is now virtually unused one year out of two. Acoustics, the study of sound, used to pull in dozens of kids who were not especially interested in science but were very interested in making their own stereo sets. For years, physics teacher Hollis Williams deftly tricked hundreds of kids into science via acoustics. Thanks to the new state standards, acoustics is gone. "In Richmond [the state capital], they're appealing to the middle and the mediocre," said one disillusioned science teacher.

The state also issued new regulations requiring every high school student to take six hours of classes a day, regardless of how many credits were needed to graduate. The state was responding to reports that some seniors were only taking a few courses and then running wild the rest of the day. But there was widespread feeling at T.C. that the state was on the wrong track. As one administrator put it, "The state's reforms are simply more of the same. Now you've got kids taking courses just to take them—regardless of whether they like or need them." Several of my twelfth-grade students who had completed almost all their high school requirements when the Commonwealth of Virginia issued its fiat were forced to sit through a few more boring classes.

A good example of the effects of this particular "reform" is the case of Karen Hagerty, a National Merit Scholar in the class of '85. At the start of her senior year, Hagerty needed only four courses to complete her requirements for graduation, and had been planning to work during the school year as an assistant in an interior design firm. But that would have meant leaving school at one o'clock and missing one of the six hours of classes suddenly required by the state. So instead she had to sign up for a vocational education course, called "cooperative office education," which allowed her to get credit for going to her job, and had to spend an hour every morning learning how to file papers and type on a word processor. Hagerty's verdict on the course, usually full of students with low academic skills, was that it was "incredibly boring."

The combination of the traditional fifty-minute class routine and the state's new six-hour rule created a frenzied, chaotic schedule for all kids, and stirred up real resentment among twelfth graders who had fulfilled most of their graduation requirements and planned to pursue individual interests in senior year. Matt Elmore, a gifted artist, had looked forward to having a free period after his art class to polish his work. Instead, he had to fill up the "empty slot" in his day to meet the state requirement. "You have ten minutes to set up, thirty minutes to do your work, and ten to clean up," Matt said.

"Art has got to be fun," says Cassandra Johnson, '85, now at Rhode Island School of Design. "But there's a stigma to it in school. You have to go to the art room and 'work' there. I usually just get started when the bell kills it. There's no time to polish—to keep working until you know it's finished. I usually end up taking it home." Cassandra confided to me that the most satisfying work she does is at the Torpedo Factory, a local art studio where she spends long hours after school and on weekends.

Given the world in which most of our students have grown up, it is hardly surprising that their tolerance for boredom seems considerably lower than that of high school kids a couple of decades ago.

Before teen-agers in my students' generation graduate, they spend, on average, 5,000 more hours watching television than sitting in classrooms. This certainly isn't all bad. Television has made us all residents of the "global village." It's put even very young children in touch with far-off cultures, taught them things about nature and the environment that no high school biology course could begin to do, and, at its best, presented beautifully packaged history lessons about man's ascent into the civilized world. It has provided educators with a tool of tremendous power. But it is a technology that also has confronted us with immense challenges which, for the most part, we have chosen to ignore. TV has changed what kids know and how they know it. A generation reared on television expects the process of acquiring information to be fast and easy. In ways that we still only dimly understand, television has affected this generation's attention span, thought processes and capacity for quiet reflection.

New electronic universes outside the school are being added all the time: videocassette recorders, cable television, and computer games. It's no longer enough just to listen to a hit song; now kids have to see it "acted out" on videotape by the stars and a chorus of seductive models. This electronic world is central to the adolescent culture. It spawns new musical fashions and even new industries, such as the thriving "video wear" business. "Some people come in with their mom's credit card and buy half the store," the manager of a local boutique in the Washington area featuring video fashions told a TV interviewer. To pay for clothes, stereos, and entertainment, my students rely not only on their parents, but also on part-time jobs which put money in their pockets. National studies report that time spent at part-time jobs has been increasing while time devoted to homework dwindles.

We applaud initiative. But we are witnessing a new phenomenon, one that Jerald Bachman of the University of Michigan's Institute for Social Research calls "premature affluence." In a society in which teen-agers have free room and board, access to a car, and maybe a parent's credit card, income from part-time jobs creates a prematurely affluent youth culture in which school is ever more peripheral, other than as a place to meet friends, and school curriculums seem ever more irrelevant.

Yet schools have only begun to cope with these enormous changes. A few computers are introduced—the new panacea—and editorials approvingly note that the schools are getting in step with the times. A few electives are added (usually to be canceled after a few years). But not much really changes. The school calendar remains what it was when America was a farming nation and there was no air-conditioning; the school day, still broken up into the tyrannical, fifty-minute unit, ends in early afternoon, just as it did when mothers stayed home. Twenty-year-old lesson plans for biology, history and English continue to be used.

There is a stubborn, self-destructive quality to the way schools cling to tradition. Nothing illustrates this more vividly than the "traditional" teaching that goes on inside "traditional" curriculums. "There's this one teacher who comes in clutching her 'lesson plan,' " says Betsy Lindeman, '85. "I have the idea it's the same one she's been pulling out of her file for the last fifteen years. If anyone asks a question or starts a discussion that takes her away from her sacred lesson plan she gets extremely nervous."

Boring, passive teachers are wedded to the test along with the text. T.C.'s Assistant Principal Bob Frear acknowledges that there are teachers who "hide behind the curriculum." "They're dispensers of information, which is regurgitated by the student in the form of a one-word answer on a ditto sheet. They either don't know or they don't care that they're boring the hell out of kids."

Brian Sullivan, class of '85, "cannot express the unbelievably maddening frustration" he feels "being required to memorize the names, works, and simpleminded description of perhaps twenty-five authors for some literature exam, when only a handful of the works have actually been read by the instructor, not to mention the students."

Yael Ksander, '84, says: "In many classes all that's going on is the transfer of information. Teachers who teach like this don't seem to realize that they're making themselves obsolete. All we really need is the textbook and some notes. In fact some teachers are a negative factor. Their attempts to explain what's in a book are so baffling. In one class the teacher is just a presence up there in front of us. We know it's alive, that it's flesh and blood, but it just goes on babbling, off in its own world, totally out of touch with what we need to master the subject matter."

More than twenty years ago, James Coleman summarized the conflict between what young people want and what classrooms usually provide:

> Modern adolescents are not content with a passive role. They exhibit this discontent by their involvement in positive activities, activities which they can call their own; athletics, school newspapers, drama clubs, social affairs and dates. But classroom activities are hardly of this sort. They are prescribed "exercises," "assignments," "tests," to be done and handed in at a teacher's command. They require not creativity but conformity, not originality and devotion, but attention and obedience. Because they are exercises prescribed for all, they do not allow the opportunity for passionate devotion, such as some teen-agers show to popular music, causes or athletics.

Coleman was saying that good schools have more to teach students than just intellectual substance. Of course they must teach students to think, to question, and to learn. But they also should help their students develop other personal qualities: determination, helpfulness to others, creativity, confidence in their own bodies. Some of this can be done in a good classroom but the classroom can never do it all.

I think T.C. has survived the competition from private schools and achieved its good reputation in the community not only because it turns out National Merit Scholars but also because, at its best, it recognizes the importance of opportunities for its students outside the classroom. Our extracurricular program is one of the school's strong suits. In 1984–85, we offered some forty-nine outside activities and thirteen major sports. More than half our students were involved in one or the other. Some 210 kids—nearly one in ten—signed up for crew. More than 200 were involved in some kind of musical group—stage band, vocal ensemble, orchestra or wind ensemble. About ninety were involved in drama, through either the two annual school plays or the three elective drama classes. Other activities ranged from forensics and debate to Russian Club and the Astronomical Society. Then there were those who were going wild over computers, or hanging around the chemistry and physics labs, working on projects of their own during lunch hour and after school.

In the fall of 1984, the school board adopted a policy that made students with less than a C average ineligible for the athletic program. The board's reasoning was that athletes would start taking academics more seriously if they had to do more than just slide through with D's. The C requirement was proposed by a black school board member who was justifiably concerned about the poor academic performance of many black athletes. Across the Potomac river in Prince George's County, Maryland, the school board established a C average requirement for participation in clubs and school shows, as well as sports. Nearly forty percent of Prince George's students were unable to qualify. Prince George's schools were soon treated to the unusual sight of coaches organizing study halls for their best players, drilling them on sentence structure instead of their running and passing game.

Such attempts to raise academic achievement unquestionably address a shameful situation. There is no excuse for forty percent of any student body to be on the brink of flunking at any one time. Yet there's something rigid about the new approach. School is not a zero-sum game in which effort devoted in one area automatically means effort subtracted from another. It ought to be possible to raise academic standards without forfeiting activities that can help develop kids' self-esteem and confidence. The conviction underlying the new rules seems to be that the basic business of school is the development of intellect, that what happens outside the classroom is expendable—not really "education" and perhaps not really "school," either. Yet what happens with or to students outside classrooms affects their performance in them. Success in extracurricular activities can translate into academic achievement.

What if we abolished sports, extracurricular activities and electives altogether? Middle-class students would continue to play the game, feigning interest in class, getting their A's and B's, going on to college—but learning no more than they do now. And it's questionable whether we'd see more motivated students from disadvantaged families.

The experience of Marina Cuadra, '84, suggests how important these "extra" activities can be in a high school education. Women's crew became her passion, but it didn't detract from her academic performance. "I have a real love–hate relationship with the sport and with the coach," Marina told me. "I don't like to think where I'd be if I hadn't gotten into crew. Most of the girls are pretty good students, and just getting thrown in with them made me realize I could do honors work if they could. Crew has helped me academically in other ways too. I don't fret over school and grades the way I used to, but my grades have gotten better.

"The ironic thing is that crew has made me feel more *feminine*. I'm not exactly what you'd call petite. I have to struggle to keep my weight under 140 pounds, and with crew I've been able to do that. It has changed my whole attitude about my body and eating. Eating is a major part of my family's life. My mother has always pushed this wonderful Spanish food at her five children. It's always, 'Eat! Eat! Eat!' If it weren't for crew, I think I'd be pretty fat and unhappy. It's helped me see there's nothing unfeminine about a woman being big. We girls in the heavyweight boats are proud of our size. We love to see those scrawny little lightweights—the ones with what the media promotes as the ideal bodies, the model types—in the weight room trying to pump iron. They can bench press about ten pounds."

The education theorist Jerome Bruner says that "we get interested in what we get good at." That states something important about motivation. Bruner argues that doing, trying, and testing come *before* getting interested. Getting good at something is the hook that creates commitment to it, not the other way around.

When Brian Françoise entered T. C. Williams in tenth grade he didn't have any special interests or talents, but he did want to make friends. First, he tried out for the musical *Hello Dolly*. The two parts he got were minor, but Geri Fillmore, the drama teacher, seemed to like his ideas and suggestions. Two months later Brian, who had never had a singing part in his life, tried out for the role of Jesus in *Godspell*.

"Seventy people auditioned. Each of us had to sing a song from the play, and I was the only one to choose 'Alas for You,' one of the more difficult numbers. I was stunned when Mrs. Fillmore chose me for the role. I know that from the outside a high school musical can look like a silly four-night thing with a bunch of adolescent egomaniacs running around a stage. But it's amazing; a thing like that can change your life! I felt the teachers recognized me now and expected things of me because they knew I had talent. I had something to live up to. Then one day Mr. Hanley came up and congratulated me. Now he always says hello. I know it sounds corny, but those kinds of things have made a big difference in how I feel about school."

Geri Fillmore thinks that drama provides a sense of community—a place for kids within the big school that makes them feel at home. Also, the plays are important as "social products that involve kids working together." Fillmore says that the auditorium is a "sanctuary"—"a place in the school that's their own." Brian Françoise agrees. "It's a home in the school for us. The auditorium and the stage and all the things we've shared there—the tryouts, rehearsals and opening nights. They pull us all together into a real family."

Kids *want* challenges and will accept risks. When senior Jill Schwab signed up for Human Resources in the fall of 1983, she was apprehensive. Jill had excellent grades and was involved in school activities, but something was pushing her to try something different. In Human Resources, students earn credit tutoring retarded elementary school children twice a week. During the first bus trip to the center where she was to meet and work with a retarded child, Jill remembers that she and her classmates were uncharacteristically silent. Jill was to tutor Nicky, a seven-year-old boy with Down's Syndrome, and she had planned a crafts lesson. She'd made a cardboard turkey and would try to get Nicky to paint it. "I was scared because I wasn't sure if I could handle Nicky, but once we started, things went smoothly. He kept saying, ' 'Urkey, 'urkey,' and he really got into the painting."

Jill came to understand Nicky's problem with putting together words in a coherent pattern. "He has all these ideas in his head and he's been so frustrated about not being able to get them out, so my first objective was to get him to put adjectives and nouns together. I worked with him a long time and finally he seemed to be improving, but I was never sure that he took what I taught him outside of class. Then one Sunday I went to Nicky's home and took him for a walk. As we were walking down the street, he pointed toward a car and said, 'Red car,' and then to another and said, 'Blue car,' and another, 'Green car.' Hearing Nicky identify objects correctly was one of the biggest thrills of my life. I felt I had helped him begin to break through his isolation."

Working with Nicky has been Jill's most important accomplishment at school. "This was one of the first things I did that was truly mine," Jill says. "I've gotten very little personal satisfaction out of my classes. Even all my extracurricular activities didn't mean that much. Like so many of my friends, I got involved in a lot of activities so colleges would be impressed by my record. Working with Nicky is so different from all that boring grind of school. With him I've had to be creative and flexible; I have to find my own solutions to problems that arise. And I've done very well with him. My teachers recognized that and said I have a special talent working with children—and I do. I've never felt so good about myself as now."

Many teachers tend to write off Human Resources as a nonessential, nonacademic frill. I used to tease my students about the "psychobabble" they were learning there. But after listening to some of my best students tell me it's the course that's meant the most to them, I've come to realize that in fact it offers education of the most profound kind.

If only each of our 2,400 students could have just one experience like Jill's, many of our educational problems would be on their way to being solved. Unfortunately, school never connects with hundreds of its students, the "silent majoritty" who are lost in the shuffle. They're often the most vulnerable: the poor, the foreign, those suffering through some recent family crisis or divorce, the newly arrived.

Marie Arnold came to T. C. Williams in September 1983, from an American high school in Naples, Italy. She tried out for the girls' soccer team but was cut, she feels, before the coaches got a good look at her. It seemed to her that the team had already been selected from girls who'd played the previous year. Then she tried out for the spring musical. She didn't make the cast. In senior year she gave up on school activities. Though she was accepted at several colleges, she was quiet in class. Sometimes I think we let her down.

It isn't always apparent who's to blame. I first met Sherri Williams in a summer school class after she'd failed sopho-more English. She was very intelligent and certainly capable of doing well in an honors course. But she hadn't "caught fire" then, and she didn't in the two years that followed, either. "Toward the middle of junior year I was barely hang-ing on," she told me much later. "I clung to Mrs. Gill's En-glish course, but senior year I had nothing to hang on to, so I just dropped out." Sherri, seventeen at the time, went to work at Hechinger's, a large hardware store. The April after she dropped out—two months before she would have grad-uated—she got married.

Sherri is somebody who "fell through the cracks." Al-though her decision to drop out was rare for a white, middle-class kid (and increasingly rare for all students), the feelings that drove her to it are all too common. In 1984–85, I had three girls in my slower-than-average English class who were, it seemed to me, typical of the hundreds of others in school whom we just aren't touching. All three were middle-class whites. None of them was involved in any outside school activities. None, I was to learn, was a member of any particular clique, and none had any real friends in school. Two were dating older guys who didn't attend T.C. All three left school by early afternoon to go to jobs, which they found more interesting than school.

It was obvious to me after several weeks that none of the three really belonged in this English track. Kim and Nicole often brought their own novels to class and read them when they got too far ahead of their classmates. Nicole was an avid fan of Stephen King and went through his novels at record speed. She claimed to have been assigned to the slow-reading track solely on the basis of a low grade at her previous school. As for Shanna, her mother explained to me that she just wanted her daughter to graduate without any trouble. Unfortunately, by the time I tried to get Nicole and Shanna switched to my honors English course, where they could have been exposed to classmates with similar abilities, they were locked into their schedules.

So why were they put there in the first place? Two of the three (Shanna and Nicole) were newcomers at T.C. Both had recently landed in Alexandria following their parents' divorces. Shanna was living with her mother, Nicole with an aunt. Both girls had run away from home the previous summer and were only just getting back in their parents' good graces. For Shanna, who had come from a small private school near Baltimore, the change to a large and unfamiliar public school had been a difficult culture shock.

Kim was coming off a series of personal setbacks that seemed to have drained her self-confidence. There had been an unpleasant experience in ninth grade when, she said, she had made a serious attempt to raise her academic sights and win acceptance from her classmates by signing up for a more advanced English course. As she bitterly recalls it, the teacher embarrassed her in front of the other students and "called my mom and said he wanted me out." By the time I met Kim, she had made up her mind to take the line of least resistance in this particular English class—a strategy, I must add, acceptable to her guidance counselor.

"It's been depressing all through high school," Kim said. "I go home and watch TV. I'm looking forward to getting a [full-time] job." Shanna describes T.C. as "scary." She recalls the trauma of her first day at T.C.: "When I went to the private school in Maryland, they assigned an older student to spend a day showing me around. Here they hand you a map of the school at the guidance department. They throw you to the wolves." She says, "The only groups that are easy to crack are the bad ones—the druggies." So, rather than fall in with them, she's made no new friends. She goes straight from school to her afternoon job at a hairdresser's.

All three of these girls have potential that isn't being brought out in school. Kim could catch fire under the right circumstances. In eleventh grade, she enrolled in a course in "office practice" at the Secondary School Occupational Center, a special facility attached to the school system for fifteen-to-twenty-one-year-olds who have dropped out or are considered dropout risks. Classes are small—usually no more than ten students—and the atmosphere is relaxed and informal. Students and teachers share a smoking lounge. Jeff Wilson, who runs the center, is more of a counselor than a principal. "Nobody gets lost here," he says. "We believe in the arm around the shoulder." Kim thrived at the center under her teacher, Carolyn Wheaton, with whom she and her mother remained in close contact after she came over to the regular high school in senior year.

A few months after Nicole joined my class, my wife and I took our dog to the veterinarian's where Nicole had told me she was working. The girl who came out to greet us was a different Nicole from the impassive one I had in class. She was smiling, curious about the dog and excited about helping us. I was glad to see her being so enthusiastic. But I also went away feeling a little sad and a little guilty that the experience of school was so uninspiring for this young woman.

In one way I feel I ought to just kick this threesome out of my "slow reading" class so that they could be challenged and perhaps stimulated. But I've developed some rapport with them, and that could be a big factor in how they get through senior year. Also, I wonder where they'd go if they left my class, since the best teachers already are overloaded.

I know there are kids "hiding out" in a lot of my classes. Maybe I've entered into what the educator Ernest Boyer calls "the corrupt contract" between teacher and student, in which the message from the teacher is "Don't bother me, attend class, keep quiet, be nice, and you'll have no hassles." But this is a complicated problem. In a class of thirty, it's almost impossible to engage everyone in a Socratic dialogue. I often feel a shy kid might cave in—perhaps drop out of the course—if I put pressure on him in front of the rest of the class. We can't be paralyzed by the worry that we're not reaching every kid. We have to take it on faith that we're getting through even when we can't see the results.

On the other hand, the big, comprehensive high school, the center of American secondary education which is supposed to have "something for everybody," all too often seems to have plenty for motivated kids whose parents know how to take advantage of what the school has to offer, but less for the majority. Because they still come to school, take tests, and eventually get their diplomas, we can easily make the mistake of thinking we're "serving" our pupils. I think we underestimate how peripheral school has become in their lives, except as a social gathering place. We get angry because they're more interested in jobs or a hobby than our "objectives" and curriculums. But we, the educators, are fixated by tests and by the obligation to cover the material. It is we, the educators, who are in danger of trivializing education.

7

Tales Out of School (II)

I'm thinking that the unit on poetry I've just taught was pretty good when Ellen Butler hands me a note on her way out of class. This young woman has been very quiet all through the course. I think, probably she's just too shy to tell me how much she's appreciated my teaching. Then I look at the note.

"If you want to know the reason I look so bored in class it's because you're presenting a one-sided view of things. You've only done a few poems by women. We're constantly getting the male view."

Wait a minute! Who does she think she is? She may write great papers and be a great student, but she doesn't contribute to the classroom discussions—and now this! As I seethe, I realize I'm feeling awfully defensive. By the end of the day I've cooled off enough to go looking for her.

"I'll make a deal with you," I say when I catch up to her. "If you bring in some poems by women, I'll do them. But you have to talk more in class."

She comes back with several poems by Adrienne Rich and Maxine Kumin, and the class, which is three-quarters girls, goes wild over them. But I'm still secretly brooding. I think to myself that the note-taker is probably surprised that this was happening. She probably didn't think a sexist pig like me would actually keep his word. But later in the year I find out accidentally that she really likes my class now—as much as I enjoy reading her papers—even though she's still quiet in class.

I decide to make Rich and Kumin a permanent part of my senior English class, and every year their poetry provokes an intense discussion—especially when we read Rich's "Trying to Talk to a Man."

Three years after Ellen graduates she sends me a book from some course she's taking at Vassar: *Daughter of Earth*, by the feminist writer Agnes Smedley. She accompanies it with another note, this one much warmer but still cautionary. It ends, "and watch out for those sexist remarks."

The representative from the Princeton University admissions office has arrived at school. I've been waiting for this.

A few months earlier, the local Princeton alumni rep had sent me a copy of a note to Guidance Director Jim McClure. The note explained how sorry he was that Princeton had turned down everyone from T.C. the previous year. He went on to explain that it must have been the "low" math score of Elisabeth Orshansky that had kept her from entering the ivied nirvana in New Jersey.

I did a slow burn. Elisabeth's "low" math score had been 630, which is well into the top range. She had 780 on her verbals, was fluent in several languages, including Russian, and had been accepted at Harvard and Stanford. It just happened that St. Agnes, a private Episcopal school attended by the daughter of the alumni rep who interviewed Elisabeth, had sent *three* students to Princeton.

I go into the conference room where the admissions woman is giving a spiel to about twenty smiling candidates. Maybe one of them is in Elisabeth's league. I sit quietly for a few minutes, but finally can't restrain myself any longer. I interrupt her.

"I'd like these students to understand something about Princeton," I begin. "Hardly any of our students except minorities or jocks have been accepted, while many others have gotten into Ivy League schools." I tell the story about Elisabeth. "She wasn't preppy enough," I say. "She didn't live in Old Town [Alexandria's section of old and expensive houses]. She didn't load up on silly activities just to impress somebody. Her interviewer acted bored." I'm really getting psyched up now, and go on to tell how Harvard had arranged to have a Russian speaker interview Elisabeth in order to assess her mastery of Russian, and how impressed Harvard had been as a result.

Everybody's stunned. I realize I've been pretty rude, but I also think to myself that Princeton will get $40 an application from these kids, most of whom don't have a prayer of getting in. For a while I thought that my outburst might have done some good; I heard that Princeton interviewers were on the defensive after that. "I think I might get in just so they can prove you wrong," the valedictorian of the class of '85 confided to me with a grin. No such luck! Princeton turned down our valedictorian. The alumni rep's daughter got in— early admission.

Pete Hawley, '82, was only sixteen when he became a senior. He was younger and maybe a little less mature than his classmates. There were long stretches when he seemed to be doing no work at all. I did my duty and gave him the D's and F's he deserved, but I made sure his bad grades didn't stand between us personally. We talked sports a lot. He was a starter on T.C.'s football team and was a sports trivia buff—the only kid I've ever met who could reel off the starting backfield of my favorite football team, the 1964 Buffalo Bills.

I realized I was dealing with a closet intellectual. Pete would usually show up the earnest grinds who were getting A's when I'd have students write in class on some esoteric poem they had never seen. I remember making a copy of one of Pete's best papers and handing it out to the class. It was sensitive and graceful and most students thought it had been written by a girl. When I revealed that the author was a six-foot-two, 200-pound offensive tackle, there were a lot of surprised looks.

Pete's performance went up and down through the year. Except for the in-class writings, he seldom scored higher than a C. Toward the end of the year, Pete asked if I thought he should take the advanced placement test in English. "Of course," I said. "Go for it."

Four weeks after Pete graduated from T.C., I got a call at home. It was Pete. "I got my AP score. It's a 5" (the highest possible score).

A couple of years later I'm at the Alexandria Y for a swim and run into Pete. He's just finished weight lifting, staying in shape for football at the University of Pennsylvania. We talk for several minutes, and I feel there's a real bond between us. I think to myself how glad I am that I didn't kick him out of my honors English course when he goofed off that first semester.

A few years ago I get a call in the middle of summer from an administrator then employed at T. C. Williams.

"Hi, Pat, would you like to come out for a drink?" I don't know the guy that well, but he's being sociable and I don't want to hurt his feelings.

It's a good forty-five-minute drive to the home. He and his wife, who is also a school administrator, greet me. Several other guests have already arrived. The "drink," it seems, is ginger ale. We talk for a while, and the host and hostess then usher us into the living room, where the host starts giving a cryptic speech about motivation, interspersed with comments about how much he and his wife dislike working in the schools, how we all dislike it, how we get no respect, how our colleagues are unfriendly.

The answer, we are all told, is to get out of teaching and get into selling Amway products. They go through a routine showing how Amway detergent works better than another brand. The host dirties a towel with shoe polish, dips it into the Amway soap and brand X, and—presto!—the Amway product wins hands down. I'm sitting there in a state of shock, but since he's over me in the school hierarchy, I listen politely.

Later I find out that several of my colleagues have been similarly "entertained."

Where is this pair now? Are they detergent executives? No, they're both administrators in the school system and are making more money than ever. The last time I checked, they were still being entrepreneurial in their spare time. They were opening a Popeye Chicken franchise.

An officious-looking woman walks into my classroom. She introduces herself as the "homebound instructor" for a student of mine who'd left class the previous week in the eighth month of her pregnancy. During the time she was with me she got an F for the first quarter and a D for the second. It was all I could do to keep her awake in class. She lost the copies of both novels I gave her. So now she would be getting one-on-one tutoring at home from this woman.

I have a free period coming up but have ten papers to grade for an afternoon class. When the homebound instructor asks for fifteen minutes to go over a detailed lesson plan for the girl for the next nine weeks, I brush her off.

"I don't have any time," I say. I tell her what novel we're reading and say the kid has it.

"She tells me she never got one," says the instructor.

"Do whatever you want with her," I say, now really angry.

After she leaves I feel pangs of guilt. I walk into the teacher's lounge and tell a colleague what happened.

"Great," she says. "I can't stand talking to those people. Get pregnant and you get special treatment." Now *she's* furious. I spend the next few minutes trying to calm her down.

We're a few minutes into class and I hear a strange cooing noise. I look around and there's a baby sitting on the lap of one of the students. It isn't the first time this has happened, and as always, I'm kind of nonplussed. There's a rule against bringing babies to school. But I don't want to embarrass the girl by asking her to take the baby out. So as I walk around I stop from time to time and touch the baby, who grabs my finger. The child looks to be about a year and a half old and is smiling, alert and pointing to the blackboard a lot of the time. The mother, seventeen, is passive and doesn't participate in class. She has great difficulty reading and keeping up, even though this is a class for poor readers.

What if?

What if I'd called that girl's mother the same day I got her message instead of stuffing the number in my pocket and forgetting about it?

The girl was in my English class and, though not a great student, was a pleasure to have in class—witty, sweet, and, from all outward appearances, happy. One day she showed up with a black eye, but I just kind of chuckled about it. Something told me it might be serious, but I got caught up in the class and then with other things. Then one day came the message to call the girl's mother. I mentioned it to the girl over lunch. She shrugged as if it was no big deal. It didn't seem to be a crisis, and the mother's call slipped my mind.

But a few days later, the girl suddenly dropped out of school. I got a note from the assistant principal saying that she'd run away from home. If she showed up I was to call him immediately.

I was surprised and felt terrible. The girl didn't come back, either. Later I learned from friends of hers that she was all right—she'd called her mother but wouldn't say where she was. But the question keeps coming back. What if?

One morning, Nader, an Afghan student who graduated with the class of '83, unexpectedly shows up in the guidance office wanting to talk to Jim McClure.

"Send him in," says the guidance director. Then Jim does a double take. Trooping behind Nader are an older man and woman followed by eight kids, ranging in age from three to eighteen. "These are my cousins," announces Nader proudly. "They arrived Saturday. I said you'd be the one to help them." It takes McClure the next two hours to register Nader's three high-school-age cousins, all of whom had been certified as refugees by the Immigration and Naturalization Service. Welcome to T. C. Williams High School. Welcome to America.

I'm reading one of the best papers I've ever seen. It deals with a James Joyce short story about a woman who controls her daughter's life, forces her into a loveless marriage, then controls the son-in-law as well. The paper provides powerful insights into the character weakness of a man who allows himself to be manipulated by a strong-willed woman.

I like the story. Usually I get discussions started on it by mischievously asking whether this isn't the way *most* relationships are. But I'm disturbed by the girl's paper. Her first three essays of the year were thin. So after class I confront her.

"Did you write the paper?" I ask.

"Yes," she stammers, tears welling up in her eyes.

An hour later, I get a phone call. It's the girl's mother wanting to see me after school. I see the girl at lunchtime, and she admits she's had a lot of help, but insists she put in some 15 hours on it over the weekend. She'd write something, then her mother would ask questions and come back with some suggestions for revisions. It went on and on.

I pick out certain phrases from the paper and ask, "Did you write that?"

"No, my mother wrote that part."

I expect to dislike the mother, but when she comes in, it isn't what I thought. The mother is successful—has a doctorate, works at a good job. I can feel the girl's pain, empathize with her self-doubt. But the mother strikes me as a very decent person. She knows she's putting too much pressure on, doing too much herself. I believe her when she says she doesn't think grades are that important. I start to feel a little teary myself. It's as if we're all caught up in "the system," where achievement and grades and success are everything. I realize I'm part of it, too—pushing my students to do well on national tests and circulating copies of the "best" papers for others less talented to see. I just feel sad.

The next semester, the girl drops the honors course.

Albert Ahern, a prominent Washington lawyer, isn't one of those parents who expects more of his kid than he does of himself. On a bet from his daughter Elizabeth, he took the Scholastic Aptitude Test. Al came to school on the appointed day, stood in line with the kids, and sweated through the exam. When the results came back, it was no contest. Elizabeth outscored her dad by 50 points on the verbals and nearly 300 on the math. Elizabeth, who's since graduated from Brown, still tells the story.

.   .   .

A new kid suddenly appears in my English class for slow readers. He's British, and it's quickly apparent that he belongs in a more challenging section. To be honest, it isn't just academics. I'm also thinking that in a more advanced class he'll meet kids who'll accept him more easily than the predominantly minority kids in Phase 2. The Englishman, who's been in the United States for only two days, seems in a state of culture shock. I try to put him at ease by telling him my wife is English. Later I take him to lunch in the cafeteria and introduce him to a group of some of my most social students. That afternoon I get him transferred to another more advanced English class and introduce him to a girl who came from England a year ago. She takes him around Washington and he makes some friends. Within a couple of months he seems a lot more at home. It's nothing much, but it makes me feel good that I helped one kid connect a little.

"Do you think they're human?"

The speaker is looking out the window toward the music wing, where about twenty-five kids, many in jean jackets or T-shirts, are standing around or sitting on a low brick wall.

"I'm not sure if they are," a classmate replies.

"Looks like *Escape from Planet of the Grits* to me," says a third.

The kids outside are called various names—rednecks, freaks, burnouts. But mostly they're grits. A girl who hung out with them last year described their common bond this way: "Boredom with school, contempt for authority, and a love of the weed. Which comes first, I don't know."

Grits feel misunderstood. "Those arrogant preppy types think our dads are all pumping gas or driving trucks, but a lot of us come from more money than they do. We just don't show it off like them," said a grit eleventh-grader.

Preppy. New Wave. Punk. At first glance, they look different. But as some students tell me, they're really pretty interchangeable cliques of white middle-class kids. Inside of a month kids have been known to go from "ultimate, clean-cut preppy" to "hard-core, down-and-dirty punk." The New Wave types, with their flashy, hi-tech fashions, fall somewhere in between. John Martone, '84, had an apt description of them: "punks who like their mothers and still take out the garbage."

The family situation has deteriorated pretty far when counselor Pat Butts hears about it. The daughter has left home after being given the option of improving her behavior or finding another place to live. Butts gets the girl into her office and advises her to ask for shelter in a home operated by Child Protective Services. The girl is admitted and things go well for a while. But soon she's back in Butts' office, unhappy and ready to seek a reconciliation with her parents.

With Butts acting as intermediary, the mother and daughter meet for dinner several times. The next step is weekend visits home, to test the girl's readiness to live under family rules. For the next two months, Butts and Child Protective Services keep in close touch with developments. Finally, the girl moves back home full time, after she and her parents sign a written contract spelling out one another's responsibilities and obligations in the home.

"On a break of this magnitude, the child and the parents can't just kiss and make up," says Butts. "There have to be some hard lines drawn up so everybody knows what the rules are." Chalk up one success story for our guidance department.

A Korean boy has been summoned to principal Tony Hanley's office. The report is that he's just knocked a classmate unconscious. The boy may have a couple of broken ribs. Yet it's all Tony can do not to laugh. The victim, Hanley knows, is a notorious bully who's frequently been in his office for threatening kids and making slurs toward foreign students. It seems the other Korean students learned that the newcomer was a karate expert and arranged for him to meet the bully, who never knew what hit him.

The Korean boy has been in the United States barely two weeks and speaks hardly any English. Hanley is trying to tell the boy that fighting in American schools is against the rules. Another Korean kid is interpreting. The kid keeps bowing to Hanley and saying something about "honor . . . honor." He says, "I take care."

"What are those cops doing out there with Hanley and Porter?" asks a guy sitting near the window in my sixth-period English class the day before Thanksgiving.

I put aside *Henry IV, Part I*, and look at the main entrance of the school. Hanley and Assistant Principal John Porter are talking to two uniformed Alexandria policemen. What convinces me that *real* trouble may be brewing is that they've been joined by Frank Holloway, our school's six-foot-three, 240-pound hall monitor, a former college football player whose sheer bulk has a curiously pacifying effect on potential mischief-makers.

For Hanley, the day has started off miserably and gone downhill from there. A few minutes after he gets to school at seven o'clock a hysterical teacher bursts into his office in tears. The kids in the student club she sponsors had planned to raise money that morning by selling M&M candies, but an administrator has just advised her it isn't permitted. It seems she hadn't filled out the proper forms. Now the red tape has finally gotten to her.

As Hanley is trying to calm her by telling her something

can be worked out, Lil Lubsen, his secretary, buzzes his office to give him the news all principals dread most: "There's a fight in the lobby."

As the upset teacher dries her tears, Hanley rushes out the door. ("Rushing" for him is really a brisk walk; if students or teachers ever saw him running or showing any signs of panic, they'd immediately start wild rumors.)

In the lobby, a crowd of screaming students converges on him. By now, Assistant Principal Bob Stoy has stopped the fight. But the combatants—four girls and the three boys they'd gotten the best of—surround Hanley to argue their cases, with a little help from their friends and supporters. Amid all the shouting, one question prevails: Where did the girls put the hat they'd ripped off a guy's head at the bus stop?

Serious fights are a rarity at T.C. When I heard that this one was a real donnybrook, I knew that girls must have been involved. In all my years at T. C. Williams I've hardly ever seen a real fight between boys. They usually just shove each other a little and see if someone will intervene before things degenerate and punches have to be thrown to save face. But the girls are real battlers. I've seen clumps of hair strewn on the floor after girls have gone after each other.

After one look at this particular flap, Hanley knows that his plans for the day are shot. The first thing to do is separate the warring factions. The three boys are remanded to Porter and Hanley escorts the four girls to his office. But as he's doing that, a boy and two girls from last year's graduating class, just back from college, come rushing up to him, expecting a big welcome. The girls hug him; the boy shakes his hand.

"It's so wonderful to see you; how are things going?" asks Hanley, who's trying to keep the four brawlers moving. "I'm a little busy right now, but come to my office later in the morning and we'll talk," he says, hurrying on.

Back in his own office, Hanley gets the girls settled and tells them to stay while he makes a quick tour of the building to make sure everything's peaceful. In the main lobby he's in the middle of hustling stragglers to class when he's approached by two more girls.

"Mr. Hanley, I know you're busy, but this will just take a second . . . " one of them says. They want him to sponsor a demonstration for nuclear disarmament at the White House. With one eye on the crowd that is still rehashing the fight and the other on the two girls, he says that the school could sponsor a forum to discuss nuclear disarmament but not a demonstration for one side or the other. That's not the answer the girls are looking for, but like most people who come to Hanley with a problem, they go away satisfied—though not necessarily knowing why.

Hanley finishes his reconnaissance run after about 15 minutes. Ninety-nine percent of the students aren't even aware there was a fight, and Hanley wants to keep it that way even if that means taking up a large part of the morning.

Back in his office again, Hanley tries to get to the root of the fight. He gets several different versions, but it seems that the first blow was struck the previous night, at the Charles Houston Recreation Center on Wythe Street, which is frequented by T. C. Williams black students. A boy punched a girl, and the next morning at a bus stop in Old Town some of her friends sought vengeance. Things escalated and came to a head in the lobby.

As Hanley listens to the overwrought girls' fragmented story of who did what first, his secretary buzzes to announce that School Superintendent Robert Peebles is on the phone. Peebles wants to discuss "the needs assessment analysis for the total school program," then asks Hanley to describe his own MBOs (central office shorthand for Management by Objective) for the school year in progress.

Suddenly the alliance of young women in front of Hanley begins to crumble as the four start shouting at one another about who did not help whom enough. With his immediate MBO being the prevention of a brawl right in his office, Hanley politely tells his boss that he'll have to get back to him.

Somehow Hanley manages to quiet the girls down enough to slip over to Porter's office, where one of the three boys is still complaining about his stolen hat. After pooling their information, Hanley and Porter decide to suspend one of the girls and two of the boys. The plan is to have them out of school by lunch, lest they stir things up again in the cafeteria.

It takes Hanley a good fifteen minutes to locate the parents. Nobody's home. Hanley advises the parents that the kids are being suspended and has three of his administrators drive the kids home in separate cars. It's now ten-fifteen, and the bell signaling the first of two lunch periods rings, presenting Hanley with a new worry that tensions could escalate in the looser environment of the cafeteria. He heads there, making sure students see that he's calm and relaxed. After an hour of working the crowd in and around the cafeteria, he feels that things are normal enough for him to salvage some of the appointments he's had to cancel and catch up on the paper work he planned to finish before Thanksgiving recess. But as he's leaving the cafeteria, he gets word through his information grapevine of student tipsters that "the A-Team is on its way."

It seems there'd been trouble the previous Saturday night at a dance at the Gum Springs Recreation Center in Fairfax County. Several T.C. students had been in a fight with students from Prince George's County, across the Potomac River in Maryland. On Tuesday, a car full of Prince George's kids came to T. C. Williams to try to settle the score, but were chased off by superior numbers of our students.

Now Hanley's tipsters have heard that the vanquished Prince George's students have enlisted the help of the A-Team, a gang of older street dudes from southeast Washington. The word Hanley gets is that they will soon be arriving to bring doomsday to T.C. "Keep walking, talking, and smiling—visibility, visibility," mutters Hanley to himself as he leaves the cafeteria. "If we can hold the lid on until dismissal everything will dissipate over the weekend."

He now has a difficult decision to make. He knows that reports of this kind usually are just talk. But what if just this once there's a real rumble? What if the A-Team, whatever it is, *does* show up? Shouldn't he have police on hand? Or would the presence of police hurt the school's image? Will members of the community driving past the school think we're turning into a blackboard jungle?

Hanley puts prudence ahead of image and calls the Alexandria police. But before he even gets a chance to reach his office, he's grabbed by a teacher. "There's a drunken boy in my class, would you smell his breath?" she asks Hanley. The principal administers his personal breathalyzer test—a close-up whiff of the boy's breath. The kid passes. "Smells like mint to me," says Hanley. The teacher, crestfallen that the principal thinks the kid is sober, goes back to teaching. Hanley goes to call the cops.

By now it's eleven-thirty and the second lunch hour is in full swing. It seems to Hanley as if half the student body is milling around in front of the school when the two squad cars pull into the driveway. (Other police cars are stationed along roads leading to the school to watch for carloads of suspicious people.) Hanley and Porter greet the men in blue, and while Porter stays in front with them, Hanley does a brisk walk around the school grounds chatting with the various cliques—punks, preppies, jocks, grits, musicians—each in their favorite lunchtime habitats.

Suddenly Hanley's beeper goes off and he heads quickly back to the front of the school, where the police have just received a message that two cars full of suspicious-looking young men have been stopped by two squad cars near the Baskin-Robbins two blocks from school. It's just the Prince George's County boys—no A-Team. They're being frisked and soon will be escorted by the police out of Alexandria across the Woodrow Wilson Bridge. "Just like the cowboy movies I used to see as a kid in Maine," Hanley mutters to himself. "Get out of town and don't come back."

Hanley spends what's left of the day in perpetual motion, dropping in on classes, keeping visible. He looks in on a Russian 3 class, where a small circle of students are discussing in Russian some poems about the Moscow winter. "The extremes in this place are amazing," Hanley says to himself for the thousandth time.

As he continues his rounds, everyone seems to want a piece of him. The "just one minute" routine is played over and over. A teacher complains about dirty bathrooms; a visiting parent wants to discuss her son's grades; a class officer asks about this year's prom site; a janitor advises him he can't find the source of a gas smell that drove a teacher and her students out of a classroom that morning. And he pays a brief call on a student who fainted.

At exactly one fifty-five, the final bell signals the end of school. But as Hanley is saying goodbye and wishing a happy Thanksgiving to the mobs of students boarding the buses, a bus driver reports a fight. Hanley scrambles aboard the bus, visions of a major rumble swirling in his head, only to find two small, meek-looking sophomores arguing over the right to a window seat.

Back in his office, Hanley tries to catch up with piles of unfinished business. He signs teachers' leave forms and checks, sets the date for the prom, dictates two memos, and reads letters. Thanks to the antics of a tiny handful of students that day, he's got at least three more hours of paperwork ahead of him. At three, he puts the undone work in his briefcase, says goodbye to his secretary and heads for Nags Head, North Carolina, for the holiday.

All the educational studies about what's wrong with high schools agree on one thing. The difference between good schools and bad ones often comes down to one individual, the principal. T. C. Williams has a potentially volatile mix of students. It's a place that could unravel without a sensitive and flexible person in charge. People who saw Hanley walking around smiling and shaking hands may not have thought so, but this was a day he earned his $50,000 a year. He kept this school with all its diverse elements running smoothly, and he did it in his characteristic way. Hanley always worked hard at making it look easy; he made it look so easy, in fact, that some of the "get tough" reactionaries in the system complained that he wasn't doing enough. Yet his charm, wit and natural grace helped pull T.C. together during its most difficult years, and earned him the respect and affection of the school community. Those same qualities also stirred up great envy and resentment among his earnest colleagues, who, despite all their courses in school administration, just weren't in his league.

Driving south on Route 95 for his holiday, Hanley argues about the day's events with the rear-view mirror. He's well beyond Richmond before the tension begins to fall away, and he realizes next Monday is four full days away.

8

Teachers

The Russian writer Anton Chekhov once told a story about a man who tried to teach a kitten to catch mice. Whenever the kitten refused to give chase, the man beat it. After the animal grew up into an adult cat, it always cowered in terror in the presence of a mouse. "That," said Chekhov, "is the man who taught me Latin."

The story describes all too well what happens in some high school classrooms. Some teachers are horrible; their methods and personalities turn students against learning, leaving scars that can last a lifetime. Even at a good school like T.C., there are those whose work is downright destructive to students' intellectual growth.

A teacher is at the blackboard, back to the class, working out the answer to a problem from last night's homework assignment. Two guys in the rear of the room play poker. Music drifts softly from a portable radio. Still another young man sleeps with his head on his desk. Several other students are doing homework for the next class. After nearly half an hour at the board, the teacher arrives at the answer. A student quickly points out that it is incorrect. The teacher checks over the work and acknowledges the mistake, but gives the excuse that the noise in the room made it impossible to concentrate.

Another teacher is giving students the "silent treatment." The teacher writes a word on the blackboard and asks the class for the meaning. When students volunteer answers, the teacher says nothing. Students try other definitions. More silence. The instructor stares out at the class, starts grading papers and examines the attendance book. On some occasions the silent treatment has lasted quite a few minutes.

At the front of another classroom, several students are having a private discussion with the teacher. The other fifteen or so kids slide their desks slowly toward the rear of the classroom. Soon they are all bunched up in back, chatting, doing homework, filing their nails. The teacher goes ahead with the discussion, ignoring the group at the back until the bell rings.

It would be a mistake to think that bad teaching is related to inferior knowledge or intelligence. I know of one teacher who knows the subject well but has no idea what the students are up to. One day, a third of the students have their heads on their desks, fast asleep. Girls in a group are talking loudly about a party. After twenty or so minutes, one of them says in an audible voice, "Hey, is the teacher still talking?" Only two kids—both Vietnamese—seem to be paying much attention. "If you're not going to sleep you have to talk just to keep awake," says one of the students later. "The teacher's voice is a drone that blends in with the air-conditioner and puts you right out." There is a lot of cheating during tests. The exam questions do not change from year to year and students use answers from the previous year. Sometimes students secretly open up the teacher's grade book and change their grades.

In one class, students who feel they're not getting their money's worth decide to give the teacher a test. Week after week, their papers come back with only a check mark. They're suspicious that the papers aren't being read. Several students begin sprinkling obscenities through the writing that they turn in. One girl writes, "This is a f—— waste of time and paper." Back come the papers with the same check mark. The teacher has failed.

Every year I teach summer school I'm surprised at the large number of perfectly intelligent kids who are required to make up work they've failed in the regular year. I've had summer school students progress so rapidly that I could give them credit and excuse them halfway through our six-week makeup course. And every summer I hear them talking about the same teachers, who consistently fail large numbers. We summer school teachers joke that we should turn over half the money we make to the handful of teachers whose F's have swelled the ranks of our summer courses. Every July, the kids describe those teachers as "frustrated," "unhappy," "out to get us."

The summer school kids can be rebellious types. But many of them are having problems with growing up—not with learning. An understanding teacher at any time of year could help most of them get through, but often it's the teachers who haven't grown up. They get satisfaction from provoking teen-agers. I think especially of the plight of a very intelligent black student I taught in the summer of 1984. During the school year, he had developed a personality conflict with one of his teachers, who antagonized him so much that he finally quit coming to class. The teacher has the power and usually "wins" confrontations such as that, but teachers who "get" kids forget that the word "education" comes from the Latin *educare*—"to lead out of." It is the teacher who's supposed to lead the creative and intellectual potential out of the student!

Some teachers truly are burned out. The students know which ones they are. "I think there ought to be a big sign in the main office, 'If you're sick of teaching, get out,'" Kathy Berkman of the class of '84 once told me. "It's too obvious that some of our teachers are just hanging around waiting for retirement. And they're the ones who are turning the best students off." Kathy, now at Barnard College, was right, of course. But worse than the minority of my colleagues who are burned out are the smaller number who seem to hate kids. The guidance department knows who they are. Every fall, after classroom assignments are given out, guidance counselors are besieged by kids wanting transfers.

One student described her predicament in one class: "Last year the *highest* grade given on a test in my advanced modern language course was my C. Most of the other grades were D's and F's. This teacher treated us like dirt. She told one boy who was struggling, 'You're stupid—what are you doing here?' When I got my C, I suggested that from the grades it seemed we had not learned the subject very well, and asked for some review. She pretended not to hear. I got transferred to a class where I could learn something. By the end of the semester, more than half of the original twenty-two in her class had switched."

As a teacher who usually loves his work, I get angry at evidence of malpractice. But it has to be seen in a larger context. The few truly incompetent teachers among us are the end product of a system that for years has tolerated steadily deteriorating working conditions, discouraged the best young minds from entering, imposed burdensome bureaucratic procedures, and failed to recognize or appreciate the extraordinary commitment and dedication of most of the high school teachers I know.

From time to time, I have a bout of actually *hating* my profession. I was in one of these moods the day Paula Swanson told me she planned to become a teacher. Paula, of the class of '85, was a straight A student with the highest scores on the Preliminary SAT of anybody in her class, and a mind that could rapidly understand an entire poem while other kids were still struggling with individual lines or the meaning of a word.

One day I asked her what colleges she was applying to.

Michigan State, Madison (in Harrisonburg, Virginia), and William and Mary, she told me.

I was puzzled. "You'll get in easy," I said. "Why not apply to an Ivy League school—or Stanford?"

"I'm interested in education, and those places have good departments," said Paula.

I went wild. "Education! Are you crazy?" I asked. "Wasting a mind like yours on that! You could be anything you want."

I had this vision of her being treated like dirt by ignorant administrators and nasty kids.

"No, education is what I want to do."

I was completely stumped. How could I argue with that? I could feel one of my self-hatred bouts coming on. I wanted to tell her that, as a teacher, I'd been unusually lucky. I hadn't burned out, but many had. I felt like saying that education isn't a profession that rewards talent, that a brilliant girl like her would get paid the same as some jerk in the next classroom who's doing nothing with kids. I wanted to warn her that she wouldn't meet many interesting men in teaching, and certainly none with much money. She'd meet jocks who went into coaching or school administration because they're frustrated little boys who want to relive their high school athletic days. She'd probably meet quite a few gays— one of the few classes of people who can live decently on teachers' pay because they seldom have families to support. I wanted to warn her that some of her women colleagues wouldn't be very dedicated to teaching, but would be merely working for the pocket change of a "second income." I thought to myself, she'll probably intimidate some insecure administrator because of her brains, and he'll retaliate by finding some corner to shove her into.

I managed to hold my tongue. Later I talked to Geri Fillmore who teaches Human Resources. Geri had been watching Paula tutor retarded kids and was really impressed with her abilities. She said that Paula's lesson plans were creative and that she showed great interest and talent in teaching the handicapped. "Don't worry," said Geri, who'd probably experienced such moments herself. "She'll be writing the books, finding new ways to teach these kids, making the breakthroughs."

Why do I sometimes indulge my anger at my chosen profession in this way? A hypothetical "want ad" that was included in the 1984 Rand report on the *Coming Crisis in Teaching* suggests some answers.

> **WANTED**
>
> College graduate with academic major (master's degree preferred). Excellent communication and leadership skills required. Challenging opportunity to serve 150 clients daily, developing up to five different products each day to meet their needs. This diversified job also allows employee to exercise typing, clerical, law enforcement and social work skills between assignments and after hours. Adaptability helpful, since suppliers cannot always deliver goods and support services on time. Typical work week 47 hours. Special nature of work precludes fringe benefits such as lunch and coffee breaks, but work has many intrinsic rewards. Starting salary $12,769, with a guarantee of $24,000 after only 14 years.

At T.C., a school in a relatively affluent community, teachers start at $18,200 a year and the average salary is $33,480. That is well above the national average, but it has to be seen in the context of the high costs of housing and food in the

Washington metropolitan area. (About one public school teacher out of five nationwide is estimated to hold a second job.) I'm 45, with a wife and three children at home. We get by, but there are times when I wish I hadn't been so indifferent to money and material things. I guess that went with being brought up the child of a well-to-do doctor in an Irish-Catholic community where the priests and nuns always insisted that poverty was a virtue and that God would provide!

I chuckled about that philosophy when I got a note from Sister Yvonne, the head of my son Neil's play school at Blessed Sacrament Church. Sister Yvonne politely informed me that January's tuition check had bounced and February's was late. After Sister Yvonne's note I noticed the threadbare knee on my gray flannels and hoped it would hold through winter. The spring after that note came, I needed two loans from the Alexandria City Employee Credit Union to make it through. If it weren't for the $250 or so I get in the middle of each month from teaching night school, I'd never make ends meet. I love teaching so much I'd probably do it all over again, but I wouldn't want my children to follow in my footsteps.

Typically, my day begins at six o'clock in the morning; sometimes I head for the local YMCA for a swim. I want to be at least as wide awake as my students when I meet them for my first class at seven thirty-five. During the day, I put up with minor annoyances. Between classes, there's usually a queue at our co-ed faculty toilet. One guy seems to live in there. Some days I get a chance to catch my breath during the second lunch period, which comes at the strange hour of eleven-ten. I use the time to grade papers, work the Xerox, or see students. That's provided I don't have "cafeteria duty," where my job is to watch for fights or disturbances. In six and a half hours I "teach" more than 130 students. Twice a week I get $15 an hour for teaching night school, and

Saturdays in the fall and spring I make money teaching an SAT preparation course.

But money and "perks" are not at the root of the teacher problem. People do not enter the profession primarily for the money, but "because of something in their hearts," as Anne Wheeler, who trains teachers at the University of Chicago, has put it. The Rand study concluded that the best-qualified teachers are nearly as dissatisfied with "bureaucratic interference," "lack of autonomy," and "lack of administrative support" as low salaries. I could handle my money worries better if I felt the low-income black teen-agers in our classrooms were learning; if the bored kids I teach for two or more hours a day paid attention and were interested in school; if I felt I was part of an organization in which everybody was working together to reach a shared objective.

It sometimes seems to me that there was more *esprit de corps* at the Xerox sales office where I once worked than in my own school. At Xerox, people got recognition and praise and even bonus money for good performances. At T.C., when my students excel on the college level advanced placement test, colleagues sometimes put me down for "teaching to the test."

In fairness, it must be said that the much-heralded "teacher crisis" exists in part because of forces over which the schools had little control. In the '60s and '70s, enrollments rose rapidly because of the baby boom. Teaching staffs expanded, and schools often grabbed whoever was available. As new job opportunities opened up in the economy for women and minorities, schools found themselves competing for the best talent, and often losing. When enrollments fell again in the late '70s, hundreds of thousands of teachers were let go. It was usually the youngest and least-tenured who were cut. So public school faculties around the country tend to be middle-aged. The average age of our faculty of 170 people is forty-four. The youngest teacher in the English Department is thirty-five. And now, when a promising candidate applies for a job with us, the answer is usually the same: "no slots."

Dorothy Newman, whom local theater critics consider one of the finest theater directors in the Washington area, applied to teach English and help with drama. No slot.

Emily Rothberg, twenty-three, a graduate of Swarthmore, applied to teach social studies. No slot.

Kit Basom, who coached women's crew at a local high school and was one of our finest substitute teachers, applied to teach biology. No slot. (She was hired by Sidwell Friends, a prestigious private school in Washington.)

But what of the talent that the schools *do* hire? Often they cannot retain it, a tragedy that can only be blamed on the schools themselves. Reliable studies have showed that the brightest quit the profession first, while the least gifted are the last to go. When the Rand Corporation studied the careers of white females who went to work in the North Carolina schools in 1973, it discovered that two out of three of the teachers who had scored in the top ten percent on the National Teachers Exam quit teaching within seven years, compared with one out of three of those who scored in the bottom ten percent.

In the summer of 1984, we unexpectedly lost math teacher Marty Nickley, twenty-five. Marty had been a real asset to the school. He'd majored in math and history at William and Mary, and was captain of the soccer team that went to the NCAA quarter-finals. Despite his outstanding credentials, the school did little to make sure he stayed. He was made an assistant soccer coach and given scant hope of getting the head job, which some players and parents thought he deserved. In the math department, he was assigned classes made up of hard-to-handle low achievers, with whom his formidable size and natural rapport with kids was a big asset. Marty worked hard with these students and stayed long hours after school to help them. In the meantime, older math teachers took most of the advanced math classes because they found the slower learners difficult to manage.

Marty's youthfulness and dedication were a breath of fresh air, even though they occasionally made this old-timer feel his years. But when we came back in the fall of 1984, he was gone. The last time I saw him he told me he'd applied for a job with the FBI. He just couldn't see much future in teaching for a guy who wanted to get married and raise a family. Superintendent Peebles had been concerned enough about Marty's loss that he took the unusual step of calling him in for a personal interview to try to persuade him to change his mind. Peebles told Marty that he was valuable and needed at T.C. But by then Marty's mind was made up.

A few years earlier, we had lost Bill Dunkum, head of the science department, after he parted company with the school system over an issue that bore directly on the conditions of teaching. Bill came to T.C. in 1969, a year before I did, and quickly built a science department that was recognized as one of the best on the East Coast. I never met a teacher who put in more time or energy—or who had more influence on the school system. A graduate of St. John's College in Annapolis, he had read more literature than most of us in the English department, although his Ph.D. was in physics.

Bill was more than a master teacher; he was also a master politician. He had influence with the then superintendent, John Albohm, and with the school board. And with good reason. He was making our science department into a major drawing card for the school at a time when the enrollment of middle-class students was declining rapidly. Many parents took kids out of private schools so they could study in

Bill's science department. He pulled the right strings to get up-to-date equipment for his laboratories and hired top talent—real scientists with Ph.D.'s in their fields. Dunkum introduced tough, challenging courses, such as organic chemistry, microbiology, and physics with calculus. He also introduced electives such as oceanography, acoustics and astronomy for students whose interests went beyond their required courses.

Bill's downfall came over a matter of principle. In 1979, he fought against the school board's plan to convert T.C. from a two-year to a three-year high school. He was convinced that the expansion would cause overcrowding, and force a cutback in electives and laboratory science courses that enriched his science program. In the end, the school board voted 5–4 in favor of expanding the school. Bill's role in the fight had been too visible—and too outspoken—and the new superintendent suggested he take a leave. Bill left and was last heard from working in Hawaii. Many now feel that his warnings were prophetic. The school is more crowded, courses introduced under Dunkum have been dropped, and morale in the science department is the lowest I have seen in years.

One of the biggest factors in the morale of teachers, and one that's seldom mentioned in the media hype about the teacher crisis, is the kids they teach. I think of the English teacher who was miserable when all her students were in the slowest track. She became ecstatic when she was assigned several classes of average students. That's not surprising to me. I've politicked and maneuvered to be able to teach my three advanced English classes a day, made up of most of the brightest kids in the senior class. That's an acknowledgment that may sound callous to someone outside the education system. But most teachers can identify with my ambition.

Without those kids, I doubt I'd be as enthusiastic as I am about teaching.

When I first came to T. C. Williams, I was at the bottom of a ladder of twenty English teachers. The head of the English department assigned the top students to himself. It was useless to complain. The department head shared a house with the school system's director of personnel, who had the power to transfer teachers and generally make them miserable.

When my department head moved to another city (the personnel director left shortly before him), I still had trouble getting what I felt was my fair share of outstanding students. By then I was starting to get a reputation as a good teacher, and some of the students who normally would have gone into the advanced class of the *new* department head switched to me. The showdown came when my rival tried to keep my students from taking the national advanced placement test that spring. Since they hadn't taken an "official AP course," she argued, they must not be qualified to take the exam. But she was overruled by the principal. My kids took the test and did well. Then, in 1979, eight years after I came to T. C. Williams, the principal assigned me to two "official" advanced placement courses, despite the objection of my department head.

All this is an aspect of school politics that you don't read much about in the newspaper. But it bears directly on the teacher crisis, for teacher morale is closely related to the caliber of the kids being taught.

The reality is that teachers are tracked along with kids. Given the difficulties that schools face in firing incompetent teachers, it's often easier to assign them to the least desirable students, while the better teachers usually get the brightest. But there's a "catch 22" here. Confronted with slow learners, there is little opportunity for a teacher to improve. Teaching slow learners, people eventually get to feel demoralized and defeated. And therein lies the dilemma. The caliber of the kids being instructed is a major factor in whether a teacher feels conditions at school for him or her are good or bad. By giving the poorest teachers to the poorest students, administrators are tacitly saying that there in not much hope for either to improve.

Another aspect of poor teaching conditions that the public may not easily perceive is the demeaning, wasteful certification procedures of state governments and school districts. They seem almost designed to let mediocre teachers in while turning off those with the most potential.

In Virginia, a college student who wants to enter teaching has to compile eighteen hours of credits in education courses. That is time taken away from study in his or her major field—unless, as so often happens, the major is education. How useful are these courses, other than to professors of education, and writers of education textbooks? James Cooper, dean of the University of Virginia's School of Education, points out that six hours of credit are earned practice teaching in classrooms, and that the other twelve hours represents less than ten percent of the credits required for a B.A. degree. That's "hardly an outrageous amount," says Cooper.

However, Cooper acknowledges that there has been considerable "fluff and busy work" in the courses required to earn those twelve hours. Consider the helpful advice to be found in *Psychology Applied to Teaching*, a book used in education courses at Virginia's George Mason University, where a lot of T.C. graduates go. Under "Ways to Arouse and Sustain Interest in Learning," prospective teachers are advised to "let students go to the bathrooms as often as they (legitimately) need to. At frequent intervals, ask the students if the room seems too cold or warm . . . Don't make students attempt any activity if they act apprehensive."

I sometimes wonder what the nuns who taught me back in upstate New York would think of such educational pablum. *Psychology Applied to Teaching* apparently would have future teachers believe that feelings such as apprehension have no place in schools. Yet it is exactly those feelings and emotions that classrooms need if they are going to engage students and excite the distracted kids of the '80s.

Despite the questionable value of such courses, however, it's all but impossible to avoid getting caught up in the certification labyrinth. The tale of Mary Jane Adams, now a French teacher with us, illustrates how ludicrous the whole credentials game has become. Adams was fully certified as a French teacher in Massachusetts, where she taught for four years before moving to the Washington area. She was qualified enough, in fact, to get a job as an analyst of Western European affairs with a government agency. She missed teaching, though, and in the fall of 1983, applied for a teaching job with us at a salary cut of $4,000 a year. There was just one problem: the Virginia Department of Education would only issue her a "provisional" two-year certificate. It seemed she lacked three of the education courses required in Virginia. So, she was told, she would have to spend part of her next summer in a college classroom taking undergraduate courses in health (learning to recognize illness in the classroom), in "human growth and development" and—appropriately enough—"federal and state laws and regulations." Only when I used her as an example of the ludicrous accreditation procedures in an article I wrote for *The Washington Post* did state authorities relent to the point of crediting her for a course on regulations she took in Massachusetts.

John T. Casteen III, formerly Virginia's secretary of education and now president of the University of Connecticut, acknowledges that state regulation hasn't done much to attract good scholars, but says it has helped keep the "wholly unprepared" out. But has it? The truth is there is no way of knowing. There has never been a real competency test for the state's prospective teachers. Beginning July 1, 1986, all *new* teachers will have to achieve a certain score on the National Teachers Exam. But those already teaching are not covered by the requirement. A number, I fear, would fail. The state would be embarrassed, and school districts would have to take action, possibly forcing a nasty confrontation with teacher organizations.

Once hired as a teacher, it's easy to stay hired unless budget cuts force layoffs. It's not because the school system doesn't have the power to deny tenure to teachers. All teachers in the Alexandria schools must go through a three-year probationary period before receiving tenure. But until recently, tenure came almost automatically. If a teacher had problems, the tendency was to give him or her tenure and then "pass the trash"—administrators' lingo for transferring troublesome teachers from school to school within the system. Once tenured, it's easy to be recertified. The only requirement is to earn six hours of graduate credit every six years. In an ideal world, teachers would use this requirement to strengthen their mastery of the academic subjects they teach. In practice, most teachers sign up for the easiest and cheapest courses they can find.

Thus, once a poor or mediocre individual is in the system, the chances are he or she stays. The "pass the trash" system prevailed for years. "We have to pass the s—— around and T. C. Williams has to take its share," an assistant superintendent once told me. This attitude seems to be widespread. In one case, a teacher from another Virginia school system applied for a job in Alexandria. She had glowing recommendations from her previous school, but soon after she started teaching, students complained to the front office that the teacher was acting strange in the classroom. When our administrators called the teacher's previous school to see if the behavior had been a problem there, they admitted the teacher had been terrible. They'd concocted the glowing recommendations just to get rid of the individual. Even after our school administration learned this, tenure was granted!

I know of only three instances when an Alexandria teacher was fired, and none involved one at T.C. In 1977, a teacher took the school board to court after being dismissed for "deficiencies" that had been documented in writing over a two-year period. He appealed to an arbitrator. After two days of public hearings at which he was defended by attorneys of the teachers' union, he was reinstated and awarded a year's back pay. A spokesman for the union said it had been a clear case of the school system's not giving due process. All told, the effort may have cost the school system as much as $70,000.

"If I caught a teacher nude, engaging in obscene acts with students on the front steps, and I got it all on camera, I *might* be able to fire him or her," Principal Tony Hanley used to say. "But to document incompetency to satisfy legal requirements is incredibly difficult. With the resources we have we can only focus on one teacher a year."

Hanley complains that the Education Association of Alexandria, the local branch of the National Education Association (the largest teachers' union), "spends thousands of dollars tying us up on procedural matters, never dealing with the issue of the incompetent teachers they're totally aware of. They make it impossible to get rid of teachers who are doing intellectual and psychological harm to kids. . . . Whenever I question a teacher on performance, the teacher is in the front pew at the next EAA meeting." Hanley would joke that he ought to get a finder's fee from the EAA. But the tension between the union and the school system over such issues is not a funny matter.

The EAA does a lot for teachers. Seventy percent of those at T.C. are members. I am one of them. The membership percentage for teachers in junior highs and elementary schools is even higher. The EAA pushes for better pay, and more paid leave and other fringe benefits every time our three-year contract expires. The EAA is also there to file grievances on our behalf. At the end of the 1984–85 school year, for example, the EAA was fighting a decision of the school system to credit a teacher with only five years of previous teaching experience instead of the thirteen years she claimed. The EAA also filed a complaint with the Equal Employment Opportunity Commission charging the school board with gender discrimination against the same teacher.

However, the EAA finds itself in the same bind as other professional unions. As a trade union, it feels obligated to stand behind *all* teachers. But as an organization representing professional people it also is committed to excellence in education. Its support for poor teachers hurts the union's image with the public, and even to some extent with teachers. They resent the EAA's support of teachers who don't measure up professionally.

The union argues forcefully that it wasn't the EAA, but weak administrators who hired, promoted, gave tenure to and wrote glowing evaluations of the incompetents. Mary Jackson, head of our math department, won't join because she thinks EAA is more concerned with jobs and salaries than the quality of education being provided to young people. But Jackson feels that the administration is at least as much to blame as EAA. "Horrible teachers have been allowed to slide by for twenty years or more," she says.

Former EAA president Hazel Rigby says the union gets a bum rap: "The administrators don't know how to document

poor performance, so they let teachers stay and blame the
EAA." In seeing to it that teachers get due process, she adds,
the EAA is just doing its job. It's the school system that's
fallen down in its responsibilities.

Superintendent Peebles, a dedicated educator (he has a
master's degree in history teaching from the Harvard School
of Education and a Ph.D. from New York University), tackled the problem of poor teachers soon after he came to Alexandria from Stamford, Connecticut. "Pass the trash is one
of the games adults have played at the expense of young people," he once told me. Peebles ordered school principals to
identify and document in writing weaknesses in the performance of teachers alleged to be substandard. "I don't care
if it does cost the system forty thousand dollars in legal fees
to get rid of an incompetent," Peebles said. "In the long run,
it helps the community and the kids." One of Peebles's main
complaints was that outstanding new teachers had to be let
go when enrollments declined. The evaluation system had
been so meaningless that seniority had been the only criterion for deciding who stayed.

Unfortunately, Peebles's good plan soon began to go off
track. Starting in 1982, the school board authorized the hiring of several outside consultants to improve the evaluation
system. Barry Jentz of Leadership and Learning, Inc., of Lin-
coln, Massachusetts, was brought in to show administrators
what to look for when evaluating the classroom performance
of teachers. Next, John Garofalo and Associates of Portland,
Oregon, was taken on as a consultant. Garofalo, an ex-prin-
cipal and former professional baseball player, provided guidance to the administrators on how to spot flaws in teaching.
Garofalo stressed the importance of "classroom management." He believed that there was a right way for teachers
and administrators to use their time, down to the ways they
organized the piles of paper on their desks. He told principals

they could cut their work time in half by using his techniques.

Alexandria teachers were never consulted about any of this. And the result, I am convinced, was a loss of trust in the administration. Starting in 1983–84, I heard teachers complain about the new evaluation methods. In one case, a math teacher with a long and distinguished teaching record was evaluated by an administrator using the Garofalo guidelines. The teacher showed me how she had been written up. She was faulted on her use of time. It was noted that she entered the classroom "eating an apple." The evaluation was full of nit-picking comments and the tone was negative. The teacher was so angry that she decided to file a grievance against the evaluator.

Some administrators now acknowledge that the Garofalo exercise ended up being vindictive and not very helpful—"a one-shot deal in which somebody spends two days, comes up with a lot of superficial jargon which is just a cover for a lack of depth and understanding of good teaching techniques," I was told by one senior administrator.

In the fall of 1984, teachers throughout the school system began to feel the effects of the concerted effort to document teachers' performance. At the start of school, a memo from T.C.'s new Associate Principal Bob Yeager announced a new policy of "teacher observations and evaluations," and set down half a dozen steps that were essential to instructional success. These included the "sponge activity" at the start of each class (described in an earlier chapter), and a "closure activity" in which teachers were to ask students to summarize what had been learned. Bob noted the importance of "several learning activities" (preferably a minimum of three) to "maintain student interest and attention to task."

When I saw Bob's memo I thought to myself, "I'm not taking this." I'd been teaching for eighteen years and had received enough feedback from parents and students to know I must be doing something right. Why should I be forced to go through a set of prescribed, mechanistic procedures to satisfy the school system's need to document before the public its seriousness about improving teaching? Several colleagues and I asked English department head Mary Payne to arrange a meeting with Bob.

As it turned out, the meeting went fairly well, but we didn't see eye to eye. I complained that the daily schedule was already tedious enough for students without a "sponge activity" that required them to start working the second they sat down. Bob told me he saw my point, but added that it would be "teacher's risk" not to follow his guideline. It would, he said, be acceptable to deviate from the lesson plan if a "teachable moment" arose. Teachers left the meeting chuckling over the new cliches. Some of us felt that Bob was trying to intimidate us with jargon. To me, his implication was, "I've got the latest secret about teaching—you don't."

Other parts of the school felt the impact of the "crackdown." Yeager ordered the sign-in sheets for guidance counselors pulled promptly at seven-thirty in the morning— presumably to catch counselors who were checking in late. (The procedure was soon abolished, after Guidance Director Jim McClure half seriously warned that he might install time clocks to show how much *extra* time his staff puts in.)

Meanwhile, the classroom evaluations of teachers by administrators seemed to many teachers to be more negative than in previous years. Yeager, or somebody he'd designate, would come to class, take profuse notes—often jotting down at what minute into the hour some minor event occurred— and then file a long report that included a summary of what had been observed and a comment on the teacher's performance.

What bothered a lot of us was not the evaluations as such.

I think we accepted the premise that teachers can always get better. But we distrusted the assumption that desirable teaching procedures for every subject and for every ability group could be boiled down to a single Xeroxed page, on the basis of which a teacher's skills could then be judged. An example of this was the negative evaluation that Bob gave one English teacher. During the class for slow readers that he sat in on, students were writing letters to the editor of the local paper. Bob wrote in his formal comment that the letters should have been written at home, and that the teacher had omitted the "sponge activity" and the "closure activity" at the start and end of class. Shortly after, a local newspaper printed the student letters on a full page. It gave the students, and the school, a big morale boost to see them get this kind of public recognition.

"The evaluation process is like writing a review of a play on the basis of one or two acts," one teacher wrote. "There is no awareness of long-term goals nor any determination of whether these have been met. There is no consideration given to individual differences or the diversity of students, classes and faculty."

History teacher Shannon Derian was one of those who felt abused by the process. Derian's abilities as a teacher have often been publicly recognized. In 1983 she was presented an award at the White House as one of the nation's outstanding teachers. In 1985 she was our school system's nominee for the Virginia teacher of the year. For years I've heard students praise her seminars and lectures. Yet, when she was evaluated by a former football coach on her classroom performance, she was faulted for allowing her students to continue a heated debate on a historical issue until the bell rang. The evaluator told her she should have stopped the argument, summarized both sides and declared one of them the winner. Derian says that it's ridiculous to tell kids that one side is "right" when eminent historians disagree among themselves. Rather than stop an argument before the bell rings, Derian wants her students to go out of the classroom door arguing and take the discussion home to the dinner table.

Several teachers thought the purpose of the evaluations was to collect information with which to intimidate them, not to improve their teaching. It wasn't an entirely fanciful conclusion. One administrator informed me that there was indeed pressure from school headquarters to have some 15 percent of the evaluations come out unsatisfactory. A curriculum specialist who disagreed with these types of evaluations but was afraid to speak out claims that the purpose was to gather information for transfers, dismissals or denial of merit pay.

The overwhelming majority of teachers at T.C. wanted to see the few truly incompetent instructors weeded out. However, we could all see that this wasn't happening. Nobody was being dismissed for incompetence. Instead, the effort was perceived as a crackdown, and was demoralizing good teachers. Rather than creating a collegial atmosphere in which teachers and administrators were helping each other, the new approach was sowing distrust and suspicion. It was adversarial, and it just widened the divisions between "them" in authority, and "us" in the classroom.

National efforts are under way to improve the quality of teaching. Minimum competency tests for starting teachers are being introduced. There is talk of "merit pay" and of cadres of "master teachers." But it seems to me that much of this effort misses the essence of the teaching problem. First, it often fails to make improving the *conditions* of teaching the top priority. Second, the reformers tend to underestimate the human ingredient. Kids won't learn much from teachers they don't like or respect. If we fill faculties with good human beings who are motivated by supportive school leaders and give them the flexibility to do their jobs in the changed conditions of the 1980s, the teaching "problem" will begin to disappear.

In its efforts to improve teaching, the education establishment has been emphasizing "effective classroom management." But stressing "efficiency" reduces teachers to machines and runs the risk of sacrificing the spontaneity that makes classrooms exciting places. Words such as "delight," "humor," "surprise," and "feelings" ought to be part of an educator's vocabulary, now more than ever.

That's why there's no pat profile of a good teacher. You can't be stupid, but intellect alone isn't the key. Some of my brightest colleagues haven't made good teachers, and some who don't seem to have high IQs inspire kids. Good teachers come in all types and colors. I know some who are spinsters with forty years of service and others who are twenty-two-year-olds just out of college. I know of gay men and women who undoubtedly would be criticized by parents if they came out of the closet but are among the best and most respected teachers and administrators I've ever met. And I know of blacks from poverty backgrounds who out-teach WASPs with Ivy League credentials.

Kids can relate to emotion and genuine excitement, a fact that ought to provide some clues as to the kind of teaching needed in a decade when so many students say school is boring. Keeping a pretty "roll book," and a nice, neat bulletin board aren't what it's all about. Some of the best English classes I've taught over the years have ended in chaos—with students debating among themselves and me sliding into the background. On the best days I get so caught up in the class that I *forget* to take the roll.

The longer I teach, the more convinced I am that teaching is more art than science—that it's "more like carving marble than making cars," as Larry Cuban of Stanford University has put it. Sometimes good teaching is just a matter of believing in oneself. For years, I had my students listen to a recording of *Othello* before we'd read and discuss Shakespeare's masterpiece. I kept hearing the same thing: "The record's boring." Finally, I took this problem to my secret guru, English teacher Flo West. "They don't want that damn record—they want *you*," she told me. I took her advice. We read *Othello* out loud, dividing up the parts and discussing as we went along. *Othello* came alive and no one complained that it was boring.

This isn't to say that we do not need to develop and study effective methods for teaching. We should always be asking the question, "What works?" But methodology has to go beyond the simplistic and the mechanistic. The four-week summer teaching workshop at Washington's Folger Theater tries to do that. Noted Shakespearean professors share their knowledge of the great plays with high school teachers. The discussion only begins with the subject matter, however. The participants discuss "what works"—how can a teacher get teen-agers not only to understand but to love these plays?

We teachers need chances to share our experiences in this way. But the over-programmed schedules we follow seldom permit this. The University of Virginia's new Center for the Liberal Arts has begun to create such forums. It sends scholars into school districts to give refresher courses for teachers. These occasions also provide an opportunity for teachers to dicuss methods.

In the last analysis, though, methods don't educate kids, people do. Whenever I find myself running out of inspiration, I sometimes sit in on one of Flo West's classes. West, a drama and English major at Kansas State, was in summer stock before going into teaching and feels she's never really left the stage. She's fond of saying that she has "five performances a day, each to a different audience, and I have to be 'up' for each one."

I remember her "performance" at a first-period class for eleventh-graders. The subject was poetry—not one that is always dear to the hearts of Phase 2 kids who are reading slightly below grade level. Many teachers would have begun with technical stuff—identifying oxymorons, metaphors and similes and only later going on to the poetry itself. Not West. "Give me a beat," she commanded. A guy in the front row began pounding out a rhythm on his desk top. Others picked it up and suddenly thirty-two pairs of shoulders started to move. West began to sway and chant the first stanzas of "The Congo," by Vachel Lindsay, in time to the beat that was filling the classroom with sound. At seven-forty in the morning, West had drawn the energy out of a group of kids with little previous interest in poetry. I sat in the back of the room, awed, thinking that I could never pull off something like that.

Schools will never improve unless we have more teachers like West. No matter how good a principal is, his school will be poor if weak, unmotivated people are in the classrooms.

During my two decades of teaching, I've grown cynical about the chances of "improving" the poorest teachers. Through workshops, observing other teachers and being coached by top teachers in their subject matter, good teachers can get better. But there are some who simply won't benefit from "remediation." They lack the personal qualities to master their subjects or deal with kids. It's unconscionable for schools to let them go on. If the only way to move them out is with the "golden handshake" of a few years' pay, that would be more cost-effective than letting them remain in the classroom. Early retirement should be pushed harder for people in their fifties whose ratings are low. The Civil Service does it. So does the military, which eases out officers with mediocre efficiency reports.

Once the decks have been cleared of the truly bad teachers, schools can seek the best replacements, whether they be young men and women fresh out of college, or older people with a love and understanding of young people and expertise in their fields built through years of practical experience. An education degree or the requisite education courses should not be the principal criteria. Put the uncertified under an experienced teacher for a year and they'll grow quickly into their jobs.

A teacher shortage is fast approaching. It presents schools with a tremendous opportunity. If personnel departments hire young people who are academically qualified, motivated, and committed, we could see real improvement. New blood, more than new theories or systems of education, is the key to improving teaching. But to attract the new blood, we need better conditions and incentives. This might mean creating teaching "ranks" that could instill a real sense of upward movement and promotion. It means creating a new sense of collegiality among teachers—not just those in one department, but across departmental lines. It means giving teachers some real power in and responsibility for their schools.

At T. C. Williams, no single step would improve the morale of teachers more dramatically than really tackling the problems of poor minorities. This means acknowledging that ordinary classroom teachers operating in ordinary classrooms seldom have the training or time to make a difference with these students. Not having an impact is professionally demoralizing.

But teachers have obligations, too. We have to accept responsibility for the poor image of our profession, and try to change it. This means breaking out of the isolation of our classrooms, observing other teachers, offering praise and encouragement as well as criticism, and drawing inspiration from each other. At the same time, we need to feel that we have an interest in the quality of our school. We need a voice in the hiring of new teachers, in the observation and evaluation process and in decisions affecting the curriculum.

If we got rid of the poorest teachers and gave the rest a bigger investment in the school, not only would classrooms become more exciting, but teachers would begin to regain the public's lost confidence and respect.

9

Who's Running This Place?

The single-page handout in my mailbox was titled "CHAR-ACTERISTICS OF EFFECTIVE SCHOOLS." Underneath was written "EDMONDS/LEZOTTE."

I knew who Edmonds was: the late Ron Edmonds, a Harvard School of Education guru who had concluded from his studies of black urban schools that the amount of time a student spent on an assignment and the teacher's expectations of what he or she could accomplish were more important than the student's family background and environment. No one I talked to seemed to know who the mysterious Lezotte was.

Then followed the seven "characteristics," and a brief description of each, complete with many capitalized words and phrases.

The handout informed me that "the climate of an effective school is NOT OPPRESSIVE." In the effective school, it went on, "the principal acts as an instructional leader and EFFECTIVELY AND PERSISTENTLY communicates that mission to the staff, parents, and students. The principal understands and applies the characteristics of instructional effectiveness in the management of the instructional program."

I read on to characteristic number 5: "OPPORTUNITY TO LEARN AND STUDENT TIME ON TASK." Here I was informed that "in the effective school teachers allocate a significant amount of classroom time to instruction in the essential skills. For a high percentage of this time, STUDENTS

ARE ENGAGED in whole class or large group, planned, teacher directed, learning activities."

Examining the memo again, I saw words and phrases that seemed better suited to a directive from a factory manager than a school official.

"assessment procedures"
"business-like atmosphere"
"the management of the instructional program"
"mission"
"accountability"
"time on task"

This was the language of the "effective schools movement," which the late Edmonds and his disciples had promoted. And as I perused this new directive from on high, I felt my irritation growing. It wasn't just knowing that these cliches would have little effect on the way a single teacher approached his or her work. It was more that the memo had been issued by an admired colleague of many years. The signature at the bottom was none other than that of "R. A. Hanley," the Tony Hanley who, as principal of T.C., had laughed at the jargon-filled memos from school headquarters. In the spring of 1984 he had been promoted out of T.C. and made director of secondary education at school headquarters.

After I finished reading Tony's memo I thought to myself that it hadn't taken him long to learn how to play the game. "What did you expect?" asked a T.C. official who was also an admirer of Hanley. "Tony's gone over to the other side."

The "other side," I knew, was the "central office," the seat of power in the Alexandria schools, headquarters of the school superintendent and home of the bureaucracy that supports Alexandria's $55 million a year public education system.

Twenty years ago, the city's public schools served 17,000 students and were governed from a building the size of a large townhouse. The entire staff, from superintendent to secretaries, totaled forty people, and the annual administrative budget was $320,352. Then a strange thing happened. As the student body steadily declined to only 10,300 in 1984, the bureaucracy ballooned. In 1984, there were 105 staff and support people drawing about $2.5 million in wages and salaries. The central office had outgrown its small headquarters and taken over all but one wing of a former school, where it was rapidly filling every nook and cranny.

Some of this bureaucratic growth was dictated by the need to monitor new federal programs and state regulations. In the '60s and '70s, school systems had to accept new administrative requirements to qualify for aid to the economically disadvantaged, the handicapped and the non-English speaking. Desegregation and battles with teachers' unions also imposed new administrative and legal burdens. Every year, the Virginia Department of Education sends the central office a forty-nine-page book entitled *Calendar Reports*, which lists more than 300 reports that school headquarters has to make to Richmond during the year. Included are such items as "Application for Aid to Pay Instructional Costs for the School Community Cannery," "Emergency Immigrant Count," and "Report of Assaults on School Personnel." There are reports on the number of students eligible for free or reduced-price lunches, on the names of teachers available for service in areas of teacher shortage, on compliance with various requirements for serving handicapped students.

Still, to a lot of us who serve in the trenches, the growth of bureaucracy is a source of puzzlement and irritation. Most classroom teachers I know, as well as some principals, are unconvinced that the growth in the size and power of the central office has had a positive effect on education. We see good educators such as Hanley churning out memos or engaging in bureaucratic turf fights. We see bureaucrats who have been allowed to go on year after year with mediocre performance, while the central office preaches to the schools about excellence and effectiveness. And we can't help resenting the high salaries and posturing of the "Dr. So and So's" who sometimes seem more concerned with their title and place on the organizational chart than with the quality of education in Alexandria.

As Theodore Sizer writes in his book *Horace's Compromise*, "Constant control from 'downtown' undermines the ablest teachers and administrators, the very people whose numbers should be expanding. These top professionals are discouraged and frustrated, often to the point of cruel cynicism. With few exceptions we observe this sad fact in all sorts of schools, in all parts of the country."

Until the early '60s, we educated students without "curriculum specialists" to help us plan our courses. Department heads and teachers in each school did this. Now there are nine curriculum specialists who do no teaching at all, and three who teach only two periods a day. They cost taxpayers more than $350,000 a year. I fail to understand why department heads and individual schools should not perform most of the tasks of these "specialists." Their contact with the classroom is minimal. In fact, they shun it. A couple of years ago, on orders from the superintendent, the curriculum specialists actually were required to *teach* for two class periods a day. Several were furious. They were allowed to retreat to their think tank at the central office after the school system reconsidered. One curriculum specialist recently was reputed to have remarked, only half jokingly, that she would never go back to the classroom unless her salary were doubled. Teachers, she said, have to "work too hard."

Compared with better-paid, higher-status administrators,

the teacher occupies but a lowly place in the bureaucratic order. He or she reports to a department head, who reports to the assistant curriculum specialist in the central office, who reports to the curriculum specialist, who reports to the director of secondary education, who reports to the assistant superintendent for instructional programs, who reports to the superintendent. A situation that came up in the math department in the fall of '84 shows what can happen in this bureaucratic labyrinth. When math teacher Mary Jackson wanted to reverse the order in which she taught two chapters from the standard math textbook, it was two months before the change was approved. She had to argue her case at a meeting attended by the principal, the associate principal, and the director of secondary education, none of whom had studied math in the last twenty years. (Jackson, on the other hand, has been teaching math for twenty-five years and is chairman of her department. In the spring of '84, twelve out of fourteen of her students taking the national advanced placement exam in calculus qualified for college credit.)

The career of Robert M. Harper, a senior Alexandria school official, shows that it is possible, given the growth of bureaucracy, to move steadily up in the system without going near a classroom for years. Harper came to Alexandria in 1966 after teaching several years in Waynesboro, Virginia. He first taught and coordinated T.C.'s distributive education program, which arranged for students to receive on-the-job training in stores and other workplaces. During the '70s, Harper briefly served as acting principal of T. C. Williams, but most of his jobs were in the central office. In 1969 he became coordinator of adult education. Two years later he was named director of vocational education, a job that had not existed when he joined the school system. In 1978 he was promoted to superintendent for educational facilities and vocational education. Two years later, this job was split into *two* jobs, both paying over $50,000 a year, and Bob took one of them, that of director of educational facilities.

In the summer of 1984, Peebles appointed a new person to that position and named Harper executive assistant for public relations and special projects—yet another newly created post, this one paying $51,000 a year. According to Peebles, Harper was to "create links with the business community." But how much PR did the school system need? We already had two suave New Englanders, Peebles and Hanley, doing a great job of stroking egos all over the community and state. And at the time the new position was created, the school system already employed a PR officer.

Harper says he liked teaching, and left in part to "get a handle on vocational education and push for more voc ed programs." But he acknowledges that money was also a factor. Until the pay of administrators and teachers is comparable, Bob says, people are always going to be leaving the classroom for higher-paid administrative jobs. He saw an opportunity to get in on the growth of Alexandria's school administration. "I edged my way out of the classroom," he says. "I went from three classes, to two, to one." In 1968 he quit the classroom altogether, a career strategy that plainly paid off.

What is the significance of this to teachers who are overloaded with 120–150 students, who are on the go all day, and, in the case of younger teachers, earn less than half what Harper does? It leads to cynicism, and, justly or unjustly, tends to strengthen the conviction that the school leadership is a private club that plays by its own rules, manufactures jobs when they are needed and generally exists apart from us.

This feeling, I fear, is only strengthened by the spectacle of administrators chasing after degrees that entitle them to be called "doctor," but don't necessarily enhance their value to the school system. Of the eight top officials in the central office, three (including Harper) have obtained doctoral degrees from Nova University of Fort Lauderdale, Florida. The Nova degree is fully accredited by the Southern Association of Colleges and is recognized by the state of Virginia. However, Nova degree recipients are not required to take comprehensive examinations, to pass proficiency tests in foreign languages or statistics, or attend classes on the university campus for a year, as is the case in many traditional doctoral programs. Many of the requirements can be met by mail, and residency can be satisfied by attending two six-week summer sessions.

Why are titles and degrees so important to individuals in the educational bureaucracy? More important, what is the connection between advanced degrees and leadership? Can hustling after degrees improve the quality of education provided to Alexandria students? As a teacher, I honestly do not feel that my doctorate of law entitles me to any special standing with my students or peers. Sometimes I wonder if I really deserve the extra money I get for having a doctorate. I feel I ought to be judged on how I teach, not on the piece of paper I was handed eleven years ago. But in the bureaucracy, titles and degrees are badges of power.

In 1984, I received a letter from Executive Director of Personnel John DuVall (a former social studies teacher and elementary school principal, and another holder of a Nova doctorate), advising me that I would have to take an additional six hours of courses to be recertified as a teacher in Virginia. When I asked for a one-year extension, DuVall denied the request, after telling Peebles my postponing the courses would have resulted in a "gig"—a demerit—from the Virginia Department of Education.

The only institution with the power to check the growth of the central office, and the authority to see to it that the community is getting its $2.5 million money's worth from it, is the school board. Board members I've interviewed say that "poor Bob" Peebles, the superintendent, is saddled with "dead wood" promoted by his predecessors into senior posts. One board member says administrators in the central office "operate on a cover-your-ass philosophy. . . . That's the only way they *can* operate, since they serve at the pleasure of the superintendent." Yet many teachers and administrators in the schools feel that the board is part of the problem—that the tendency is for the board to defer to the recommendations of the central office on important issues. Board members insist that they do confront the administration, but do so behind the scenes. Board members told me that they recently forced the central office to bring in an outside consultant to investigate "the incredible mess in the personnel office." However, some board members admit that it's very easy for the central office to "snow" them, unless they make a concerted effort to find out what is going on.

The board, in our local system of government, and, I would guess, in many others, operates under a number of limitations. Its members are appointed by the city council, which retains the final, and decisive, say over the school budget. The majority are civic-minded people who devote long hours to the school. But some board members seem to have their eyes more on higher political office than on the schools. Two current members have run unsuccessfully for city council and, in the election of 1985, a former board president was reelected to the council. The desire of a few ambitious board members to stay in the public limelight politicizes educational decisions and provides a constant temptation for them to meddle in administrative matters as a way of exhibiting their activism.

Tensions between the board and the school bureaucracy tend to be private but intense. Administrators complain that the board is often parochial in its concerns when it should be dealing with big issues, and more interested in politics than education. The tensions beneath the surface are evident at board meetings, at which the members sit on a raised dais, above the table reserved for school administrators. "Like the Nuremberg [war crime] trials," quipped an administrator. Most of the time all of this is foreign to me. I've never had the time, nor—I'm embarrassed to say—the interest to inform myself thoroughly about the work of the school board. In that, I suspect, I'm typical of most teachers and school administrators. We're intimidated by the board, yet cynical about its role. This is a sad situation, for if there are going to be any real changes in education, school boards and those of us in the schools are going to have to understand each other and work together.

The school superintendent often finds himself caught between his own staff and the board, which hired him in 1981 and gave him a mandate to improve relations with the community. The outgoing superintendent, who had had the thankless task of closing and consolidating half a dozen schools, had aroused the resentment of city council and school board members, as well as teachers.

In many respects Peebles turned out to be an ideal successor. He established good personal rapport with community leaders, and made clear that he meant business about improving educational quality. Within three years he had introduced several promising innovations, including performance incentives for *administrators*, an initiative that had been opposed by some of the entrenched bureaucrats. In the first speech I ever heard him make, Peebles made clear his strong commitment to the humanities and to good teaching. "Children do not learn in boring classrooms," he said. Soon after that, he began taking steps that he thought would upgrade the quality of both teachers and administrators. But, as I have written, the evaluation system that eventually was put into place failed to rid T.C. of incompetents or motivate teachers. Instead, it strained relations between teachers and administrators. I believe it failed in good measure because the administrators who had the job of executing Peebles's ideas were poorly prepared to do so. And, to be frank, many of them have neither the teaching experience nor the personal qualities needed for their jobs.

This brings me to the matter of leadership. Many of the administrators in Alexandria's secondary schools are former *coaches*, and most of the others have had only brief sojourns in the classroom. There is an explanation for this phenomenon. In the '60s and '70s, decades of unprecedented unrest and instability in the schools, the need was for officials who could keep order, make sure kids got along, and deal with the community over such volatile issues as desegregation, busing, teacher strikes and bilingual education. Also, the schools needed people who could carry out dozens of new state and federal regulations. School systems turned to individuals with proven ability as doers, organizers, peacemakers, and, above all, politicians. Persons with some visibility in the community were especially welcome. Coaches, particularly football and basketball coaches, were sought for their ability to keep order, deal with the public and get things done. According to a state education official, about 70 percent of the state's school principals are former coaches.

John Porter, who succeeded Hanley as T.C.'s principal, has a background similar to that of many principals. He first made a name for himself handling troublesome students and troublesome schools. In the '60s, after a brief (two-year) stint as a social studies teacher, he ran a school "crisis center," which handled unruly students who had been kicked out of regular classes. Later he took over the principalship of two Alexandria lower schools where there were discipline problems, and in that job won high marks from the community for restoring order.

During this period, school principals increasingly were drawn away from the classroom, toward administrative, political and legal duties. Many people have forgotten that "principal" once was an adjective modifying a noun: "teacher." The British concept of a school head as principal teacher is now all but forgotten. However, it is high time it was reinstated. We still need individuals to pay the bills, make sure the buses operate, create class schedules, handle the mountains of paperwork and keep unruly students in line. But while those people must have power, they need not be principals. We need principals whose primary concern is teaching and learning.

A new concept that seems to have great promise is already being tried in Virginia, at Varina High School, near Richmond. There, an administrator for school operations handles the managerial duties, leaving the principal free to visit classrooms, coach his teachers and do some teaching himself. With John Porter's full support, a group of teachers at T.C. is now looking at the Varina experiment for possible use in our school. And Porter has made known that he'd like to be more involved in the classroom, and less saddled with administrative burdens.

Perhaps this initiative will once and for all take Porter out of Hanley's shadow and help disburse the atmosphere of intrigue that has prevailed at T.C. since Hanley left and Porter took over. We teachers were, as usual, never consulted about this leadership change, and were informed only after everything had been decided. (People in the central office have told me it's naive to think that teachers would ever be consulted about such a change.) Perhaps because of the way the matter was handled, rumors began circulating almost immediately. Why had Hanley been moved so suddenly? Or had it been in the works for a long time? Was he "on the way out"? One rumor had it that he had been kicked upstairs and given two years to find a new job. Another suggested that Peebles had brought him into the central office to balance the fabled influence of Assistant Superintendent Arlene (Mickey) Moore. Or had Moore actually engineered Hanley's "promotion" in order to put her own candidate, perhaps Porter, in as principal of T.C. and move Hanley, a rival, into a job immediately subordinate to her? My own theory is that Peebles needed a confidant and someone who shared his philosophy of education. And of course Hanley could improve the poor image of the central office.

Nevertheless, the speculation about the role of Mickey Moore was to be expected. As Superintendent for Instructional Programs, considered by many to be the number two position in the school system, Moore was considered by many teachers to be nearly as powerful as the superintendent.

Moore had arrived in Alexandria in 1956. A Mormon who grew up in Crescent, Utah, and started as a small town teacher in her home state, Moore was funny, gregarious, volatile and completely unafraid to speak her mind. She occasionally would describe herself as a "Jack Mormon"—the kind who smokes and drinks on social occasions. At Hammond High School, then the community's brand new senior high, Moore quickly distinguished herself as an outstanding teacher. Hanley himself has called Moore "one of the best teachers I've ever observed." During the consolidation of high schools in 1971, she switched to T.C. and taught for two more years before being promoted to the job of Assistant Principal in charge of discipline, under Hanley.

Hammond High School had become a junior high as a result of the consolidation, and in 1974 Moore was made its principal. The school had been riven by racial tensions and lack of discipline, and the faculty was demoralized. Moore, with the help of John Porter, then one of her assistant principals, turned the situation around within a year. She convened meetings with parents and was visible in the halls, often with an arm around a recalcitrant student. One day, the story goes, a girl was swinging a club outside a classroom and had several staff members cowed. Moore just walked through the crowd, put her arm around the girl, and drove her home.

In 1978, she was called to the central office and made assistant superintendent for administration. The day she announced she was leaving Hammond, students and teachers alike were in tears.

Hardly anyone in the Alexandria school system is neutral about Mickey Moore. I've heard male administrators complain bitterly that she "shoots from the hip." But I've also heard teachers and parents say that "if you want to get anything done, go to Mickey." Over time, as myths about her proliferated, she built a power base that included friends from her Hammond days who now were scattered all over the school system, and parents who were thankful for the job she had done over thirty years. Gradually she gained a reputation as somebody who rewarded friends and punished enemies.

The contrast between Moore and Hanley had long been obvious to everybody. Both have charisma, but their styles are different. Moore can be blunt and abrasive, but also compassionate. At Hammond and T.C. she was frequently seen reaching into her pockets, giving money to kids who were broke. She sprinkles her conversation with outrageous one-liners, often making herself the butt of her quick wit. She is a doer who gets the dirty work that the superintendent doesn't want. Moore frankly admits that her favorite jobs were as teacher and principal, but that she was drawn to the bureaucracy by the prestige it offered. Hanley, with his good looks, silvery hair and a Maine accent that often makes him sound like John F. Kennedy, has a "star quality" about him. Easygoing and gently persuasive, he is the consummate school politician. Despite this relaxed style, Hanley provided leadership for the teaching staff. His personal sense of security communicated itself to the rest of us. He delegated, and knew how to protect his staff from undue meddling and interference from "downtown."

Frictions between him and Moore went back to 1973, when, for one year, she was an assistant principal under Hanley, and is said to have complained that Hanley was not tough enough on teachers or kids. "I represented the liberal, laissez-faire philosophy; I think she was angry that I kept succeeding with it," Hanley says. Friends say that Moore still laments the passing of the "old" Alexandria system and retains the loyalty of former associates who feel likewise. She often referred to T.C. as "the university on the hill," and to Hanley as "the chancellor."

Once Hanley moved to the central office, however, he and Moore were thrown together as unlikely allies in a new palace intrigue. Frictions developed between Moore and Personnel Director DuVall. According to several reliable sources, Moore wanted more say in hiring and other personnel matters. Hanley strongly backed Moore, although he was wooed by DuVall, Harper and their allies.

"Jim Akin [Director of Research and Planning] puts a Swiss flag on his door," I was told by an insider. "He just wants to stay out of the politicking."

It is really a tragedy that talented teachers and principals such as Hanley and Moore get drawn away from schools and mired in the politics at school headquarters. The dilemma is this. To rise in the system, a teacher has to give up teaching and become a manager—a principal. Then, to rise further, it's necessary to abandon the school altogether, and, sadly, to engage in turf struggles and PR games that often just make trouble for the people left behind.

As things stand now, a lot of people at school headquarters are unhappy. Good administrators are unhappy with the many others who have been promoted beyond their depth. An atmosphere of backbiting and intrigue prevails. "Most people over here are miserable. We all put on this big act like we're one happy family but we're not. If a corporation had the low morale, the backstabbing, the inefficiency and the lack of vision that we have, it would soon be out of business," one top official told me. Another official complained that the central office never seems to follow through on anything. Every year the teachers are presented with a new plan that has nothing to do with what went on the previous year. "No wonder the teachers laugh at us," said the official.

It pains me to think of all the talent we have, and to realize that as a system we are drifting. The central office seems to confuse public relations and issuing cliché-ridden directives with leadership. Until we get real leadership, teachers will continue to shut their classroom doors and do their own thing, and we will continue to drift.

10

What Reform?

By 1985 T. C. Williams High School was beginning to feel
the effects of the latest spree of "reform" to which politicians periodically subject American public schools. Virginia's Legislature was passing new laws and the Department of
Education was cranking out regulations affecting what we
taught and how we taught it. The reforms continued an emphasis on measurement: the measurement of the performance of teachers as well as of students, usually with
standardized tests.

The state's Board of Education decreed that new teachers
would have to attain a minimum score on the National
Teachers Examination. And, in the spring of 1985, an 18-
member team from the state's Department of Education
descended on Alexandria to determine whether we were
complying with the Virginia Standards of Quality and Ac-
creditation Standards. The team cited one principal for failing to fly the state flag in front of the school even though the
requirement actually had been dropped from the Ac-
creditation Standards in 1983.

Some requirements seemed just plain petty. Because of
three snow days in the winter of '84–'85, T.C. had to call
back tenth- and eleventh-graders for one more day of classes
after graduation to complete the 180 days of school required
by state law. "School didn't end, it just kind of disinte-
grated," one official commented. Other interventions by
state government were more fundamental. As I've already
described, popular science electives were cut from the cur-

riculum so that our science department's limited staff could comply with new Virginia requirements that all students take two full years of math and of a laboratory science instead of one. The state decreed that every student, including seniors, be in class for six hours a day, even if it meant signing up for "filler" courses such as "office management." There was no appeal from such rules. It was clear that power was shifting away from our local jurisdiction and that the state government intended to impose on us its concept of school reform.

A new publication of the Virginia Department of Education, *Standards of Learning Objectives for Virginia Public Schools*, was becoming the Bible of the state's curriculum reformers. The new standards were, in many respects, a positive step. They would provide continuity in curriculums year in and year out. They would shift the emphasis away from covering large amounts of material to the attainment of specific skills. The standards' authors (who included teachers) took the position that it was more important for students to develop some reasoning abilities than to rush through all of American literature, from the Pilgrims to J. D. Salinger.

The reservations of teachers had to do with the seemingly rigid plan for executing the standards, and with the potentially nightmarish bookkeeping requirements. They listed literally hundreds of things that teachers had to do at specific points in students' education. For example, eleventh-graders were to "explore the relationship between style and meaning in literature." I chuckled when I thought of my slow-track students, who could barely follow the facts in a simple story, discovering how "stylistic devices such as organizaiton, tone, diction, figurative language and sentence structure . . . relate to meaning."

The reforms reached all the way down to kindergarten.

The state expected grammar schools to develop "a formal identification process" to discover "gifted" students—but, at the same time, local school districts were warned against racial, economic, or ethnic discrimination in the screening procedure.

How did we get to this point? To answer that question, one has to examine where American public schools have been coming from.

In the late '70s, schools began to feel the backlash from the previous two decades of social turmoil. We came under fire for poor academic results, and lax discipline. By the end of the decade there was the "back-to-basics" movement, which favored restoring lean, old-fashioned curriculums composed of a few "traditional" subjects. This was a reaction to the perception that schools were offering too many electives and "frills." There was also the movement to restore prayer in the schools. It was responding, I think, to a perception that schools had stopped teaching basic American values and had become unduly secularized. By the early '80s, the public focus on the schools had completely shifted, away from using them to open up opportunities to minority groups, towards improving educational quality.

Those of us in the school trenches had trouble understanding what was happening. We were going about our business, doing things pretty much as we always had. It was true that SAT scores were declining nationally, but they had been doing so for nearly twenty years. At T.C., many of us felt that we were offering a richer education to students able and willing to take advantage of it than had been available two decades earlier. There were far more challenging, college-level courses than the high school I attended in the '50s. What we did not understand was that while we had been inching forward, everything around us had been changing at roller-coaster speed.

In 1983, the report of the National Commission on Excellence in Education reported on the educational "crisis" in cataclysmic terms. In its pamphlet, *A Nation at Risk*, it concluded that the economic security of the nation was threatened by deteriorating public schools. This report was followed by others with less apocalyptic rhetoric but the same underlying message: America's public schools required broad change. However, unlike a number of national studies that were done in the '70s, the new round of reports said little about the social and economic context. For example, they gave scant attention to the enormous impact that changes in the American family had had on schools. With few exceptions, they focused solely on the academic achievement of the student in the classroom. The implied goal seemed to be "improved output," not "better-educated people."

The new findings and recommendations were quickly seized upon by statehouse politicians all over the country. There was a rush by state legislatures to pass new laws. Some states began requiring "minimum competency" tests for high school graduation. In 1983, California passed a sweeping educational reform measure that offered large cash rewards to schools that raised test scores, while at the same time imposing drastic changes in curriculums, testing and teacher evaluation procedures. In Texas, Dallas computer magnate H. Ross Perot led a high-visibility movement to upgrade academic instruction and downgrade sports and extra-curricular activities.

At the same time, local school systems discovered that the quickest way to regain public confidence was to present a facade suggesting that modern management techniques were bringing things back under control. Inevitably, this set up conflicts between classroom teachers in the trenches, and the "reformers" at school headquarters and state capitals. The fact was that we teachers had seen reforms before. This time around, we had our doubts about the wisdom of defining good schools in terms of quiet halls, or good teaching in terms of compliance with rigid, mechanistic guidelines.

Almost forgotten in the race to impose new requirements were the studies of schools done a decade earlier. In 1972, sociologist Christopher Jencks published his controversial book, *Inequality: A Reassessment of the Effect of Family and Schooling in America*. Jencks came to the surprising (and still much-disputed) conclusion that schools actually have rather little impact on the IQ or the later occupational status, job satisfaction, or economic position of their students. If all high schools were equally effective, Jencks concluded, the academic inequality among twelfth-graders would not change much, and disparities in their subsequent attainment would change less than one percent. Family background, conditions in the home, the neighborhood, genetic attributes and other factors all seemed to Jencks to be more important in determining what happened to individuals in life than schooling.

This really was not a particularly radical insight. Although there certainly are exceptions, most schools that I have seen are no better or worse in terms of *academic* results than the students they serve. Year after year, high schools such as New Trier in Winnetka, Illinois, Langley in McLean, Virginia, and Stuyvesant in New York City turn out large numbers of National Merit Scholars and garner many Ivy League acceptances. Everybody talks about how "good" these schools are. But, of course, much of what is perceived as good about them has to do with the abilities of their students, children, for the most part, of highly educated parents.

Nevertheless, many people were outraged at Jencks's con-

clusions. They found them terribly fatalistic and negative—
a put-down of schools and an excuse for teachers to cop out.
Aside from the fact that the liberals turned out to have been
overly optimistic about how much of the imbalance between whites and blacks that schools actually could redress,
a careful reading of what Jencks said leads to a different interpretation. Jencks *wanted* schools to be good, but good for
their own sake, rather than as a means to some distant end
such as high-paying jobs or acceptances to medical school.
"Looking at schooling as an end in itself rather than a means
to some other end suggests that we ought to describe schools
in a language appropriate to a *family rather than a factory*,"
Jencks wrote. It isn't necessary to accept Jencks's research or
conclusions to appreciate the wisdom in those words. He
was saying that schools should be humane, caring institutions, not in order to achieve some quantifiable result but
because the children and teen-agers attending them deserve
that kind of support and respect.

Unfortunately, that does not appear to be the view of
many who are now busily "reforming" education. Instead of
attempting to define accurately the real needs and concerns
of children and families, the reformers, led by politically ambitious governors, state legislators, and state education officials are following their own agenda. Instead of trying to
make schools more like good families, they are attempting
to make them more like factory assembly lines, and casting
their reform efforts in terms of making America more economically competitive.

There's a rich irony here. Output-minded school reformers, not to mention many of the administrators in my own
school system, want us to believe that they're borrowing
their ideas from the hard-nosed business world. They're fond
of business language—phrases such as "management by objective." Yet the language actually is from a vanishing era in

American business. Business is not searching for excellence these days just through better control and management. Rather, corporations are stressing human potential. "How well" has begun to replace "how much" as the ethos of corporations attempting to increase productivity and become more competitive. This has involved new appreciation of the human element in the workplace. Companies have been abandoning the "bosses know best" management techniques of the 1950s in favor of Quality Circles, and workplace democracy. These techniques, some borrowed from the Japanese, recognize the importance of involving workers and employees in decisions—of giving them a stake in change.

Oddly enough, in view of the fact that state reformers seem to think they are borrowing a page from business, the new educational requirements have been something of a dud with corporate America. In the most important statement that it has issued on education in the '80s, the influential Committee for Economic Development (representing most Fortune 500 companies and some others) made clear that more was needed from high school graduates than academic "smarts." It said: "*First*, for entry level positions, employers are looking for young people who demonstrate a set of attitudes, abilities, and behaviors associated with a sense of responsibility, self-discipline, pride, teamwork and enthusiasm." Schools, the report said, have a responsibility to help develop traits such as honesty, reliability, cooperation and competitiveness in their students. The report made a strong pitch for sports and extracurricular activities, which, it said, can "reinforce scholastic pursuits." A recent report of the Business Advisory Commission of the Education Commission of the States came to similar conclusions. Chaired by Governor Charles Robb of Virginia, the report points out that many high school graduates "are not very interested in work. They show little ambition on the job. Their behavior keeps employers from hiring them and forces others to fire them. It may be that the most important contributions of school for these youths are not academic skills and knowledge students acquire, but the habits and values that schools also impart to youth. Schools must become better at instilling in students a sense of responsibility, self-discipline, reliability and a capacity for working harmoniously with others."

The educational reformers seem to be operating on somewhat different assumptions about what is needed. As Larry Cuban of Stanford University has written in a telling critique of California's educational reforms:

> Remote control of schools and classrooms has failed in the past; it is a design for failure and a recipe for future dissatisfaction with teachers and school administrators . . . the vision of school improvement offered in California is that of an accountant. No sense of what teaching is, no awareness of larger social goals of schooling, and no sense of the ways in which adults and children grow while learning intrude on the implementation of SB 813 [the main reform legislation].

John I. Goodlad, whose *Study of Schooling* extended over a decade, has found nothing particularly new about the various reform initiatives. "They involve a 'get tough' approach combined with a dose of elitism," he wrote. "Course requirements in basic subjects are to be extended, textbooks are to become 'harder,' with less watering down to the lowest common denominators of student abilities."

Educator Theodore R. Sizer, former headmaster of Phillips Exeter Academy in Andover, Massachusetts, wrote in his book *Horace's Compromise* that "less is more" where high schools are concerned. One important idea mastered, one concept understood, one novel or play studied until its themes and characters are clearly grasped—these can be worth more than dozens of "credits" that signify courses taken and material "covered." Yet many of the new state initiatives seem to believe that everything in schools can be quantified and measured to achieve the desired end. Double the number of laboratory sciences required to graduate, and what do you get? Students whose mastery of science is twice as strong as it was formerly? Not necessarily. As Sizer writes, "Master plans for cities, states and the nation that standardize instruction are certain to be inefficient; no one set of procedures can conceivably serve most students well."

Instead of piling on more requirements, we need to ask a more fundamental question: How can we help kids learn to *think and reason*? Why do so many of my brightest students have difficulty writing? The reason, I suspect, is that in our obsession with "requirements" and with "covering the material," we seldom have time to help kids exercise their thinking abilities. We desperately need to slow down, to give us time to consider what, exactly, we are trying to achieve.

"Less is more" applies equally to the bright, the unmotivated and the slow. Bright, hard-working students don't need more requirements. They need more flexibility to choose stimulating electives or more free time to pursue their own interests. Keeping them busy with more classes isn't the best way to draw out their natural talents and creativity. The *unmotivated* won't be turned on by more requirements, either. What they need are better teachers in their present courses, as well as classes that are more interesting, challenging, intellectually provocative and—yes—relevant to their own experiences than most now are.

"More" certainly won't improve the dismal plight of students who read, communicate and compute far below their grade level. More for them will lead to further humiliation and alienation, possibly even to a higher drop-out rate. A kid who can't handle even one watered-down laboratory science course won't benefit from two. And more won't address the real obstacle to their achieving in school: an attitude that what they do in class has no significance for their future.

Politically, it is not easy to argue against the kind of changes that are being imposed on us from on high. Teachers who find fault are open to the criticism that they're stuck in a rut, or afraid of "higher standards." And it's easy for parents and voters to be taken in by "experts" who are pushing "excellence," "higher test scores," and "teacher accountability." Parents, I suspect, by and large support the "get tough" approach being pursued by state governments. Often insecure about the quality of their own parenting, frequently worried about their children, they can easily latch onto the banner of tougher standards as a hope for restoring order and control in a troubled time. But I believe that in their hearts they know that education is more complicated and that, if offered an alternative, they would support it.

Until now, the "experts" have owned educational reform. However, the best judges of what needs to be done are communities, teachers, families, and kids themselves. In preparing this book, I've learned that my students *do* understand the problems of education. They have good ideas about improving schools. But they also doubt that their views count. They're cynical about an educational bureaucracy that seems remote from their classrooms and their lives, and which seems anything but interested in instilling a sense of cooperation and partnership. And they understand that an economic system, in which most new jobs are unskilled and low-paid, has a vested interest in keeping schools as they are.

This has been a book by one high school teacher about a single American high school. I cannot speak for other teachers.

I have my own preconceptions and prejudices, which I bring to my teaching, as to the writing of this book. No high school in the nation is exactly the same as mine. And yet I am sure that teachers and schools have *common* concerns and needs. I believe that T. C. Williams High School, which is oustanding in many respects, succeeds and fails in much the same way as most other schools. Unique as each school is, each confronts a similar range of problems.

For example, I do not believe that most schools are serving blacks and minorities well. Alexandria's statistics, like those for many other school systems, demonstrate that these children still are academically far behind the white and the economically advantaged. I do not agree that, in general, our public schools have made America a "nation at risk." But I do believe that a whole generation of American *blacks* is at risk because of their inadequate ability to communicate and compute. This is a threatened minority requiring emergency help. By the year 2000, one-third of public school students will be minorities. In allowing the totally unqualified to graduate, schools become part of the problem. They prove to young blacks that society has only low expectations for them.

Second, I do not believe that we adequately challenge and stimulate the most creative and gifted, or that we motivate the silent majority that is bored and indifferent. We have to find ways to make schools more exciting, useful and—yes— relevant to young people. Otherwise schools will continue to be of secondary importance in their lives.

The first step in making schools more useful and exciting is to make them more challenging. The eduational reformers are not wrong to be pressing for higher standards. It's just that they have overemphasized grades and scores, and put too much faith in such things as longer school days and more courses. We do have to get kids to raise their sights. But me-

chanistic solutions are no solutions. At this stage, there is
no real evidence that the so-called reforms being imposed on
us from outside are really demanding that much more from
kids, other than that they spend more time in class. But I believe kids would respond to what they perceive as genuine
challenges to their creativity, intellect and endurance, when
posed by teachers they know respect and care for them.

We have to find alternatives to the deadly, daily school
routine. Sophisticated lab sciences need more than fifty minutes to be worthwhile. I could accomplish more teaching my
advanced English students for ninety minutes, three times a
week, than I do now in our daily fifty-minute sessions. More
than most parents realize, schools are organized to serve the
needs of those who run them. The school calendar, the
school day, and even the school curriculum have changed remarkably little since America was an agricultural nation.
Our school year is still built around the requirements of an
agrarian society in which the labor of students and teachers
was needed for summer harvests and there was no air-conditioning to keep summer classrooms cool. The school day,
which ends in Alexandria at one fifty-five, is still organized
around the fifty-minute time block, which was invented for
an era when schools were the principal source of information
for kids and covering the material was important. Neither
the school year nor the school day is suited to the needs of a
society in which most mothers work, houses are empty after
school, and the main source of information for many students is television, electronic media and other students, not
the classroom.

Making schools more exciting will require redefining
what is truly "basic" in a high school education. Is not character growth, the study of ethics and values, service to others, and development of creative powers part of a good
education? In his book *High School*, Ernest L. Boyer of the

Carnegie Foundation for the Advancement of Teaching proposes that a new course unit be required for high school graduation: a unit of community service. In proposing that, Boyer was, I think, attempting to broaden our concept of the basics.

Could we make schools more exciting without compromising our effort to raise academic standards? It could be done. We could bring in volunteer drama teachers, put on more plays, take the school into the community to help the old and the handicapped, and bring the community into the school so that the elderly and the specially knowledgeable could share their experience and wisdom. (Many of these things are happening in isolated schools and school districts.)

Why can only thirty or so students enroll in Human Resources, the course at T.C. that works with handicapped kids? Why not open a dozen Human Resources classes? As I write this, there's a revolution in dance in this country, with Michael Jackson, break-dancing and video-rock. But there is no dance program at T.C. It's not "traditional" to have one— and anyway, aren't such things only for high schools of the arts? But what better way to bring energy and excitement into school than through dance?

Finally, I do not believe that we give the hard-pressed families we serve all the support they need. I am not advocating that schools assume responsibilities that must be parental. But we have to acknowledge forthrightly that the American family has changed in the last twenty years, and so have its needs. It is a reality that a third of households with school children are headed by a single person. It is a reality that the majority of mothers now work, and must work to sustain family incomes. And it is a reality that a youth culture with drugs, early sex, alcohol and sophisticated electronics challenges the authority of parents and teachers. These developments are forcing schools and families to become closer partners than ever before. And like good partners, they need to define their expectations of each other, candidly and clearly. Only by working together can schools and families confront school absenteeism, cheating, alcoholism, drug abuse and teen-age pregnancy.

In the future, good schools will, I think, resemble good families in their caring qualities. They will be more organized and active in their caring. English teachers routinely will be counselors as well as instructors. Faculties will share information about students. Math teachers will know which of their students are doing well in history, and which are going through the stress of a parental separation or divorce. Cooperation between parents and teachers of the kind that I described in Chapter 3 will be common. Schools will become bases for families to share experiences with other families and, if necessary, get help with their parenting. These kinds of schools will get better academic results than the often impersonal schools we now have. When students feel that several teachers know them well, and also know their parents, the tendency is to work harder if for no other reason than to please all the adults concerned about them.

T. C. Williams and other Alexandria schools have begun to consider, and even to introduce, innovations that address some of these needs. Our school superintendent made public the low test scores of blacks, a step that required considerable courage. Subsequently, he asked for the help of the Urban League and black community leaders to map a plan of attack. As I complete this book, the superintendent is setting up a tutoring program in which adults and high school students will help kids who are identified as falling behind. Principals have been asked to identify teachers who have had special success working with minority kids. They could become the nucleus of a teacher corps available to work with minority students before they slip too far behind. Also on the drawing board is a program to help the parents of very young children learn parenting skills.

Other innovations are under consideration. As mentioned in the previous chapter, Alexandria teachers and administrators are studying an experiment at Varina High School near Richmond, Virginia. Among the many Varina innovations being considered is one that would create teacher ranks, as in the civil service and military, with increased duties and responsibilities, as well as higher pay.

It goes without saying that good teachers and administrators hold the key to good schools. Recruiting and retaining these individuals requires, above all, providing good conditions in which they can work. As I have written, no single step would improve the morale of T.C. teachers more than really tackling the problems of our low-achieving, low-income students. We are professional people who care about results. Our failure to reach these kids is utterly demoralizing.

Improving the conditions of teaching also means leaving more time in school for things that are truly important: periods of quiet study, extended discussions with students, comparing notes with other teachers and counselors. The fixed, lock-step school day is based on the premise that, without it, a small number of incorrigible troublemakers would create mayhem in the halls. For the sake of teachers as well as students, we need to start from scratch in shaping a school day that will serve well-defined goals, instead of making it carry the load of a hundred different requirements.

It is up to us, the teachers, to bring about the changes we want. We cannot remain isolated in our classrooms. The closed classroom door can protect us from criticism, but it also shuts off feedback from other teachers, allows private grievances to fester and weakens us as a profession. As I was writing this book, T.C.'s faculty council instituted a voluntary program in which teachers from *different* departments are paired and observe each other teaching. I am a partner of a *history* teacher. And why not? We both feel we've learned more from each other than from all the evaluations we've had from administrators. When we offer criticisms of each other's moves, it never seems threatening. And the experience makes us think critically about what it is we do. As I was completing work on this book, the faculty council was planning to go further. It's discussing the possibility of having teachers *swap* a whole day's classes!

Our department has many unused resources. I think of Jan Riviere, who grew up in William Faulkner's hometown of Oxford, Mississippi. Faulkner shopped in her father's jewelry store. She's an expert on Faulkner and his milieu. But in their concern about covering the material and sticking to the lesson plan, English teachers seldom ask Jan to share her observations about one of America's greatest novelists.

Once we start communicating better with each other, we may be able to recover some of the power we've lost over the educational direction of our schools. Why shouldn't teachers take over the hiring of new teachers? It wouldn't preclude having the principal or his representative involved; but it would put responsibility for the quality of teaching back where it belongs: with teachers themselves. Most school principals and superintendents would, I think, welcome a chance to share responsibilities of that kind. As things stand now, they are held accountable for the quality of education in their schools. In truth, they have little control over what happens in the classroom. Most of them are too caught up in the "government by crisis" of running a big school. Some just aren't qualified to recognize or evaluate good teaching.

I am advocating "power to the teachers"—but not the kind that has become associated with teacher walkouts and strikes. The sort of empowerment I have in mind has at least some support in high places. Virginia's former Secretary of State for Education Casteen has noted that state regulation "has frequently withheld from teachers a legitimate measure of self-determination, insofar as most states *exclude teachers from the licensure boards that set teaching standards.*" (The italics are mine.)

Casteen, a scholar of eighteenth-century literature and writer of short stories, was a rare Renaissance man in the Commonwealth's education establishment. And it seems to me that he was on the right track in pinpointing the problems facing the teaching profession as follows:

> Apologists for the [recent] trends in regulation speak of concern for new [student] populations, enhanced managerial effectiveness, and clearer lines of accountability. The facts, though, are that such developments do not make the occupation of teaching more attractive, and that it is not all clear that the managerial authorities in whom greater control has been vested have the training or knowledge of academic subjects necessary to enhance teaching.

Tightening the regulatory controls over local school districts clearly has not succeeded in its "managerial" objectives for improving teaching. We still have bad teachers, still turn away qualified people, still lose good people to different lines of work. As teachers on a government payroll in a period of budget cuts and rising admiration for the private sector, we are increasingly suspect.

Yet thousands of truly superior individuals teach in public schools. They are the foundation on which the schools can build in the future. What should count in a teacher is knowledge and love of his or her academic subject, concern for kids and ability to motivate them. Courses on education methodology too often have little to do with the essence of teaching.

Over the next five years there will be an enormous demand for new teachers as enrollments start to reflect the baby boomlet of the late '70s. Now is the time for schools to seek out the lawyer who is turned off by the monotony of writing wills; the mathematician who is frustrated by work in a big corporation; the poet who needs money to support a family; the idealistic young college graduate who wants to help the disadvantaged. But finding and recruiting these people as teachers is not enough. We have to create conditions in the schools that will nurture and retain such people. This means making schools a new kind of institution that will embody the qualities of good, nurturing families as well as educational institutions of real excellence.

During the writing of this book, some people told me that "you just don't understand." I am sure some who have read it will agree. Some parents may think that I am insufficiently sympathetic to the difficulties of raising kids today. Blacks may view my discussion of the abysmal academic performance of so many black students as insensitive. Still others may find me unduly cynical about such things as school administrators, federal aid programs and fellow teachers. (On the other hand, many parents, teachers and administrators have told me that I'm much too easy on the central office.)

If I have learned anything from writing this book, it is that I am a small cog in a very large and complex machine. My information *is* incomplete. When I began showing drafts of this book to administrators in the school system, I was told by several that I was naive, and did not see "the big picture." This sometimes led to feelings of futility. Occasionally, during the writing of the book, I felt that the wisest thing to do would be to set it aside and retreat to my classroom, where I *knew* I could have some effect. At times of discouragement, I would think that maybe significant improvement in the schools really was impossible. Maybe the children of motivated, successful parents would always do well and the children of the poor, disadvantaged, would always have problems. Maybe improvements (to quote that favorite cop-out) would, indeed, "take a few generations."

Yet I was left, finally, with a glimmer of optimism. If an ordinary high school teacher could report openly about the shortcomings he sees in his own school system, if he was allowed to question higher-ups in the system, and if they were interested in *his* views and perspectives, then perhaps the obstacles to better communication, and, ultimately, changes in the system, were not so great after all. In talking to teachers, coaches, principals, parents, school board members and state officials, I did not find as much resistance to new ideas as I had anticipated. In fact, I found that many of these people shared my own exasperation with the status quo, and my own conviction that America should and can have better schools. I came to the conclusion that the barriers between teachers and administrators, school board members and principals, English departments and science departments, coaches and drama instructors and so on and so on are not so formidable as they appear. In fact, they may exist mainly in our own minds.

American education may be an impregnable fortress that will always resist real change, but a local school system is not like that. It is made up of identifiable individuals who will respond if faced with facts, prevailed on with common sense and provided with good ideas. Knowing this, I have to believe that we are closer to achieving better schools than we may realize.

Epilogue

My Kids Are Leaving Me— Again

Nowadays I make my June farewells to students by writing them notes on the blackboard.

A couple of years ago I was checking the roll for the last time when I suddenly got choked up. I made a quick exit, returned, but had to leave again. The next year, confident I'd be able to control my emotions, I started to tell a fourth-period class of seniors how much I'd enjoyed teaching them. I got about five words out and had to stop.

Another time I was collecting the last set of tests when it hit me that this would be the last time these kids would come together as "my" students. I could feel the tears starting, so I turned and pretended to look for papers on my desk. Finally, I grabbed some chalk and scribbled a note on the blackboard: "You've been one of the most talented, wild, fun classes I've ever taught. Thanks for a great year." As I finished writing, I thought of a line from T. S. Eliot: "It is impossible to say just what I mean."

In September, none of the new seniors who show up are "my" students. But of course those strangers always do become my students. And too soon after they do, they're ready to leave me—again.

Every June, my mind fills with images of classes past.

I think of the class of '83. Now *that* was a group that we could boast about. It sent more than twenty students to the

211

nation's most selective private colleges and captured all sorts of academic awards. The class of '83 had school *spirit*. Its members were eager to participate in class and join the student government.

Then there was '84—an "off" year, some administrators said. What they meant was that '84 didn't show as much leadership and academic achievement. Its members were more laid back, to put it charitably. Laid back and proud of it. "Mellow." "On to the system." "Low key." Those are words and phrases members of that class happily used to describe themselves.

"We work as hard as we have to and then stop," a member of '84 once told me a little haughtily. "We're more Falstaffian—more Dionysian than Apollonian," said another, trying to convince me he'd read his assignments in Euripides and Shakespeare. One '84er who was accepted to a top college after sliding through high school admitted with a wry grin that he felt as if he'd accomplished "the ultimate rip-off."

"It was an electric feeling to play the game and beat the system," he confessed. "When I got the letter [of acceptance] I started laughing. I felt like I'd pulled off the big swindle!"

School newspaper editor Eric Fusfield, who was going off to Columbia University in the fall, said summing up his class was easy: "We're just plain lazy."

I remember Paul McNeill, who had the highest combined verbal-math SAT score in the school. Paul seriously considered not going to college in the fall and playing in a local jazz group instead. And I remember Howard Hunter, whose sole extracurricular activity was Frisbee. Howard's one of the smartest kids I ever taught. But ask him how he planned to use his talents and he'd casually reply, "I have no idea."

The girls in '84 did better academically, but I saw the same qualities in them. They were less "high school"—that is, less cliquish, more individualistic, and in some ways more creative than the usual types. They were remarkably uninterested in status. Girls from that class turned down Harvard, Stanford, Vassar, Columbia, Sarah Lawrence, and the University of Chicago for less well-known schools. Those schools, they said, "offer more of what we want."

Recalling Carolyn Skolnick always makes me appreciate that individualistic streak. She graduated with a grade point average of 3.8. But most of her friends weren't from the Honor Society, but from Pink Static, the area's adult Frisbee team, which competed in national contests. Skolnick was the only high school kid on the team. The rest were engineers, law students, and government workers. Skolnick never even went to the senior prom. Instead, she went out to dinner with her friends from Pink Static.

As a teacher I sometimes get mad at kids with the '84 attitude. But there's a part of me that admires their kind of individuality, independence, skepticism, worldly wisdom and casual humor.

Looking back, I chuckle over the chutzpah of one former student of mine, a junior who was asked by a girl a year ahead of him to go to the senior prom. He took her to Roy Rogers for the ceremonial dinner before the big dance.

Maybe the qualities of individualism and nonconformity that so often annoy school people actually hold the key to a kid's ultimate success in life. Prince Hal's remark in *Henry IV, Part II*, "Let the end try the man," is a favorite of mine. I think kids like what it says about growing up, for Shakespeare makes it clear that the experiences of a wild and rowdy youth prepared Hal for the heavy responsibilities of kingship.

High school is a place where mistakes can be made—maybe even *should* be. We school people forget that too often. In high school, the costs of failure are still low. Later, the price will rise. So who is to say who is better prepared for the future—the obedient grind or the free-spirited experimenter? Years of teaching have persuaded me to be cautious about leaping to conclusions when predicting the future of seventeen- and eighteen-year-olds.

As I think about next year's students, I tell myself I won't forget last year's. I hope I taught them something, though it's always hard to know for sure. I think I turned some on to poetry—at least they told me so. I know the writing of a few improved—probably not because of anything I taught them but because I scared them at the start with low grades! I know some of them experienced the power of a play, if for no other reason than that I ordered the tickets and lined up the buses to take them to to the Kennedy Center to see *American Buffalo*, and *Noises Off*, and *Death of a Salesman*.

But in the end, there comes a time for teachers to stop torturing themselves with thoughts about how they could have done better and just let go. Sometimes that's hard. For me, it was never harder than the day I learned of the suicide at college of one of my favorite students. I thought, if I'd been there I could have talked him out of it. But then I realized that part of my job as a teacher is, finally, to let go.

Of course I want to see all my kids fabulously successful. I want to see Kelly Slough dancing with the New York City Ballet, and John Hendrickson discovering the cure for cancer, and Patty Spencer a judge and Cindy Bauer getting her third Tony award and Dirck Hargraves in his second term in the Senate and Lindsay O'Connell displaying her paintings at the East Wing. I could go on with eighty-three more wishes. But what I really want to tell them at the end of each year is that I don't give a damn what they do, even if it's being a high school English teacher, as long as it brings them, in the words of poet Philip Larkin,

> . . . a skilled,
> Vigilant, flexible,
> Unemphasized, enthralled
> Catching of happiness . . .

Acknowledgments

There are many people who were essential to the creation of this book. First and foremost is Dan Morgan. Without his help in writing, organizing and thinking through the issues of education, *Tales Out of School* would never be. Dan has been totally selfless, getting little recognition, while giving invaluable assistance both with this book and with *The Washington Post* articles. For his wisdom, patience, inspiration, friendship and dogged endurance during this project I am profoundly grateful.

When I handed in my first article to *The Washington Post*, Bob Kaiser, then the editor of the "Outlook" section, said, "You've got material for a book here." I thought Bob was just being nice to the nervous teacher who was about to start telling tales about his school in one of the country's largest newspapers. For his encouragement, his unerring judgment, and his prodding—"No! You can't have an extra week to finish that article. I want it now!"—I am deeply indebted to Bob.

How can I truly thank Madeline and John Anderson? They really started all of this by suggesting to Dan Morgan that I might be the teacher he was looking for to report from the front lines of a high school. I thank Madeline and John for the faith they had in me, for their sage advice and for their marvelous wit over the course of this project. To Joel Garreau—thanks for the title and for the classic one-liners (the printable and the unprintable) that made my visits to the *Post* such fun.

I cannot imagine many bosses in any profession allowing an employee full access to their operations and then full freedom to write whatever he wanted. But Robert Peebles, Tony Hanley and John Porter did that and more with me. They gave of their time whenever I wanted it, and they gave me the benefit of their insights into the workings of T. C. Williams and the Alexandria school system. Even at those times when I must have seemed to be a loose cannon on the deck, they never once tried to inhibit my freedom. These three superb educators knew that our system was a microcosm of every school system, that we had nothing to hide, and that by letting things be brought into the open Alexandria and all school systems could profit.

I owe special thanks to Jerry Bracey of the Virginia Department of Education. His assistance with the facts as well as with the philosophy of education at the highest levels in the state was invaluable. Also of great help in this regard were Margaret Marston of the Virginia Board of Education, the Honorable Dorothy McDiarmid of the Virginia House of Delegates, Jim Cooper, Dean of the University of Virginia's School of Education, and Kenneth Bradford of the Virginia Department of Education.

Thanks to all the teachers, administrators, secretaries, parents, hall monitors, school board members and others who helped me in so many different ways, especially Jim Akin, Costella and Harry Burke, Toni and Earle Baughman, Ferdinand Day, Bob Frear, Joe Gauld, Larry Gladieux, Lois Hair, Jack Henes, Jean Hunter, Mark Howard, Juanita Illera, Carol LaSasso, Lil Lubsen, Jim McClure, Melvin Miller, Mickey Moore, Joan Myers, Otha Myers, Roberta New, Mary Payne, Hazel Rigby, Jan and Don Riviere, Charlotte Stokes, Arnold Thurmond, Jane Turner, Pam Walkup, George Webber and Bill Yoast.

There was no single group that helped me understand

T. C. Williams or the issues of education more than did my students. There were many whose names are not in this book who gave me immeasurable assistance.

Lastly, I wish to acknowledge my dear wife Angela and to thank her for all the sacrifices she made so that I could be free to write. Her advice, her good humor and her love saw me through from beginning to end.